Advance Pra
Prosody in England and Elsewhere
A Comparative Approach

"In the catholicity of its examples, the breadth of its range, and the wit of its commentary, Dr. Malcovati's treatise on prosody is a valuable resource both for the student and for the general reader."

Dr. Thomas Chase, University of Regina

"To write about the structure of poetry for a non-specialist audience takes a brave author. To do so in a way that is readable, in fact enjoyable, without sacrificing scholarly standards takes an accomplished author. People who wish an accessible book on how poetry works will be grateful that Dr. Malcovati is a brave, accomplished author."

Dr. Frank Anshen, State University of New York

"Irreverent, amusing, and full of good solid information, Leonardo Malcovati's work on prosody simultaneously entertains and edifies. With an impressive range of historical examples drawn primarily from Western European poetry, the book is an excellent reference work and an equally good read. It can be dipped into to look up something specific or read at more leisure simply for pleasure."

Dr. Janice Broder, Bloomsburg University

PROSODY IN ENGLAND AND ELSEWHERE:
A COMPARATIVE APPROACH

by

Leonardo Malcovati, Ph.D.

Gival Press

Arlington, Virginia

Published by Gival Press, an imprint of Gival Press, LLC.

For information please write:

Gival Press, LLC, P. O. Box 3812, Arlington, VA 22203.

Website: *www.givalpress.com*

First edition ISBN 1-928589-26-X

Library of Congress Control Number: 2003109736

Cover art: "Kings Reflected" Copyright © 2005 by Casimir.

Format and design by Ken Schellenberg.

Acknowledgments

My unending gratitude goes to:

Guðmundir Sigurdsson for his inestimable help with Nordic prosody

Mieke Koeppen Tucker and Afra Saskia Tucker for their patience in the tedious work of correcting the manuscript

Ana Fernandez for her help in the translation of the Spanish poems.

Special thanks go to all those that kindly allowed me to use copyrighted works and namely:

Carlos German Belli for his villanelle 'Llevarte quiero dentro de mi piel'

José Rollán Riesco for the poems 'Las moscas' and 'Me dijo un alba de primavera' by Antonio Machado

Evelyn Stefansson Nef for the translation of Bjarni Thorarensen's 'Vitturin' by Vilhjamur Stefansson

Carmen Balcells for the poem by RAFAEL ALBERTI 'Los ángeles mohosos' (de SOBRE LOS ANGELES), © Rafaél Alberti, 1929, y El Alba del Alhelí S.L.

Faber and Faber and the Eliot Estate for 'The Waste Land', Collected Poems 1909-1962 by T.S. Eliot, published by Faber and Faber Ltd.

"Poetry is what gets lost in translation."
Robert Frost

Contents

Introduction

Is the Earth actually round? This spiny question nagged scholars for centuries for a reason: no one could see the shape of the planet. And this, in turn, was because no one could view it from afar. Theories followed theories, and humanity, after burning and gaoling a few forerunners, came gradually to the conclusion our planet was roughly spherical. But it wasn't until the first satellites actually took off from our planet and portrayed it from Space that those quiet, nagging doubts subsided.

Likewise, it is the Present Author's opinion that the magmatic jumble that is known today under the name of 'English poetry' cannot be understood except from *outside*, from the point of view of the various foreign influences that, through the centuries, moulded (and sometimes crippled) it. This is a rather vast topic and, in order not to write tomes over tomes, it had to be limited in many ways in this book. First of all, only a few, more directly correlated, literary traditions were considered: namely, French, Italian, Spanish, Provençal and Old Norse; anything written in other languages was only considered in passing, if ever.

Second, those aspects of poetry that concern *content* and *poetic language* were entirely ignored; this guide therefore treats mostly one thing: prosody, or rather (as 'prosody' is a murky and obscure term with too many a shade of meaning) the *phonetic nature of poetry*. Also, to make the comparison easier, the analysis was directed for the greatest part to classic pieces, those where the forms are clearer, and extended to free verse only in those later chapters where it was strictly necessary.

This said, the casual, external observer of English poetry (such as the Present Author, a Milanese gentleman) cannot but be struck by how little of it is actually indigenous: everything seems to have a point of comparison abroad, proving that a teeming cultural exchange always conjoined Great Britain and other English-speaking countries to the rest of Europe. With enough patience, the English examples can be matched with corresponding ones written in other languages that, mostly, predate them. This approach helps us consider them as *cases* of a broader trend rather than as isolated vents of national genius: this meeker conception of the matter is enough to shed light on several facts, and mainly on how full of misconceptions, unjustified pride and overt absurdities certain widespread ideas are.

Our comparison will, rather rhapsodically, consider all sides of English poetry, from verse to rhyme to form to the more subtle devices that are recognised only by the careful reader. In doing so, the Author commits to doing something that has become terribly rare nowadays: abstaining from quoting Himself, or His close friends as paragons of bardic genius. As a matter of fact, His opinion of most of the poets mentioned is extremely low on a strictly personal level and, as shall be seen, among them one will often find Villon, a murderer and robber; Spenser, who despised Italians more than anyone else in the world; self-obsessed, Fascism-supporting Ezra Pound, and many that in their life were brown noses, stuffed shirts, full of conceit or shamelessly commercial: in the end, a countless throng of people you wouldn't want to date your daughter, follow you in a back alley or sell you a used car. But none who doesn't have something to teach us.

I. Versification

There are several approaches to how verses are constructed in classic poetry; as we shall see, none of them actually works with most classic poems, but they do yield some interest (and some real examples as well).

Feet

This approach is based on a funny mistake in considering Latin prosody (which itself is not considered in this guide) and taken extremely seriously by English scholars. It comes from those times in which British poets took delight in calling each other 'Adonais' and in believing Heracles had created porridge to strengthen the Manly Virtues of England. The rest of the Orb finds this approach screwy, even when applied to English poems, while real Latin experts consume their liver in vain anger every time it is mentioned. Coming to the details, its main principle is that each verse can—and must—be split in metric modules called 'feet' and, as we shall see, this much is true. What is ludicrous is the enjoined concept (which has affected late nineteenth century English poetry not a little) that good verses should be made of sequences of equal feet, that the likes of Shakespeare strictly used this approach, or even that each classic verse may be divided into feet in a single way.

Feet are classified according to the sequence of stressed (S below) and unstressed (U below) syllables they contain; the most common ones are:

- US: Iamb (as in 'litchi', 'abduct')

- SU: Trochee ('engine', 'number')

- UUS: Anapaest ('oversexed', 'employee')

- SUU: Dactyl ('comforting', 'horrible')

- USU: Amphibrach ('vibrator', 'enchantment')

- SS: Spondee ('halvah')

Verses made of iambs only are fairly common in English, and found at times in French as well:

> The ship was cheered, the harbour cleared
> —S. T. Coleridge

> Soit biens soit maus, n'en poeut partir
> —anonymous of the Narcisse

Purely anapaestic verses often belong to humorous poetry in English, and are found mixed with other types of feet in French:

> To the horror of all who were present that day
> He uprose in full evening dress
> And with senseless grimace endeavoured to say
> What his tongue could no longer express.
> —L. Carrol

> Pour bannir l'ennemi dont j'étais l'idolâtre,
> J'affectai les chagrins d'une injuste marâtre
> —J. Racine

Other feet are almost never used alone in a verse; although Carrol's experiments have bred these two examples, one trochaic, the other amphibrachic:

> Yet, the picture failed entirely:
> failed because he moved a little

> .   .   .   .   .   .
> Say what is the spell, when her fledgelings are cheeping...

The Author of these notes cringes in horror at the very thought that purely dactylic or spondaic verses exist in modern European languages, but cannot safely deny they do; at least, He can grant they are not found easily.

Syllabic Versification

French, Provençal, Spanish and Italian, which have had enough time to solve their Oedipus' complex towards Latin's fatherhood, define metres first of all in terms of number of syllables to the last stressed one. We shall, from now on, refer to this as *the number of metrical syllables*, which is perhaps the most important concept in this whole guide; caution is recommended, since, elsewhere, the same term is sometimes used to indicate a different thing.

In terms of the number of metrical syllables, there is no difference among the three following verses (they all have ten, in case you didn't feel like counting them):

> To be, or not to be: that is the qui**z**
> To be, or not to be: that is the qu**e**stion
> To be, or not to be: that is the qu**a**ndary

These three endings are usually referred to as *masculine, feminine* and *triple*, respectively. We shall try to avoid such terms in the remainder, as the nature of the endings is usually irrelevant, as the Reader will soon realise.

In archaic poetry, the number of metrical syllables is almost the only criterion that matters, as shown by these examples:

> O amore_amat**i**vo,
> amor consumat**i**vo,
> amor conservat**i**vo
> del cor che t'ha_alberg**a**to
>
> .   .   .   .
>
> —Jacopone da Todi

(6 metrical syllables)

> Vers Deus de totas **i**ens
> aiaç dreiç chausim**e**ns,
> pietaç et merc**e**,
> et mais vos prec de m**e**,
> quar mout vos ai forf**ai**ç
> eç en diç et en **fai**ç
> eç en autra mes**u**ra
> don hai faiç mespriç**u**ra.
>
> .   .   .   .
>
> —Provençal anonymous, 1254

(6 metrical syllables)

Leres, leres, fait li hermites,
tu es pires ke sodomites,
ne chiens ne leus ne autre beste.
Je cuic, par les iex de ma teste,
s'uns chiens l'eüst tant traïné
par tantes agues, par tant gué,
si l'eüst il puichié tout plain,
et tu ne n'as mie un seul grain!
Or voi je bien que Diex te het.

.   .   .   .

—Anonymous of 'Le chevalier au barisel',
thirteenth century

(8 metrical syllables)

These fragments aren't particularly thrilling, but they prove their point quite clearly: there is no pattern inside the lines: their only common feature is having the last stress on the eighth (in the French one) or on the sixth (in the Italian and Provençal) syllable.

Similar samples may also be easily found in mediaeval Latin, but that would again go beyond the purpose of this book; if anyone were interested, he'd just have to browse the Carmina Burana to find his quarry.

Of course, the character of a poem built syllabically does depend on the number of metrical syllables in each line; actually this isn't necessarily homogeneous (counter-examples will be given later). Assuming it is, the basic guidelines seem to be:

- High numbers of metrical syllables (more than nine) form unruly verses, which require some additional constraints in the stress pattern of their inner part. The solutions chosen in classic poetry regarding this point shall be expounded in the next paragraph; there are, moreover, several exceptions to this rule.

- Verses containing more than 12 metrical syllables are infrequent.

- Verses with an odd number of metrical syllables are generally sing-songy; they were used nonetheless in some of the worst examples of mediaeval poetry, and are extensively employed in the dullest romantic 'songs' (see chapter V). We owe their introduction in readable poetry to Baudelaire and to the many among the decadent and symbolist (admitting a distinction exists among the two) that imitated him. On the other hand, these verses are the most naturally sung, and they constitute a good ninety percent of both libretti and rock lyrics, not to account for hogwash like country and pop; the difficulty in providing examples in the latter category is due to the general illiteracy in the environment, where syllables are swallowed in singing or added by means of oh-oh's and similar gargles. In classical music, one may just pick up at random:

Madamina,_il catalogo è questo
delle belle che_amò il padron mio:
un catalogo_egli_è che_ho fatt'io;
osservate, leggete con me.
In Italia seicento_e quaranta,
in Almagna duecento_e trentuna
cento_in Francia,_in Turchia novantuna,
ma in Ispagna son già mille_e tre.
—L. Da Ponte

(for Mozart's *Don Giovanni*, 9 syllables)

More Reasonable Verses

Historically, pure syllabic versification was a comfortable option during the short flare of Provençal poetry, and was used in France at least till the beginning of the twentieth century; partly syllabic metres were also employed by Italian poets during the same period. Soon, however, the need seemed to arise to stiffen longer verses in order to make them more regular. The most primitive solution is putting a stress on a fixed syllable inside the verse, thus breaking it, in a sense, in two, as shown in this example by Villon, in which octasyllabic verses are split in two equal parts:

Je suis Franç**oy**s, dont il me p**oi**se,
Né de Par**i**s emprès Pont**oi**se,
Et de la c**o**rde d'une t**oi**se
Sçaura mon c**o**l que mon cul p**oi**se.

Endecasillabo

One of the earliest applications, and one that would dominate Italian poetry to this day, and affect English and French as well, was the *endecasillabo*.

This verse is systematically defined as 'a verse of eleven syllables' by English-writing prosodists, which shows how they ignore not only Italian literature, but a good deal of their own as well. In reality, it comes in two varieties, both of which have *ten* metrical syllables and usually contain a caesura after the first mandatory stress:

- *a minore*: has a fixed major stress on the fourth syllable, none, or a weak one, on the sixth and another major stress on the tenth:

  Consiros v**ei** | la passada fol**or**
  —Dante

  Là ver l'aur**o**ra | che sì dolce l'**au**ra
  —F. Petrarca

  Urnas pleb**ey**as,| túmulos re**a**les
  —L. de Góngora

  Friends, Romans, c**ou**ntrymen, | lend me your **ear**
  —W. Shakespeare

- *a maiore*: has a fixed major stress on the sixth syllable, none or a weak one, on the fourth and another major stress on the tenth:

  Souvenha vos a t**e**mps | de ma dol**or**
  —Dante

  Aura che quelle chi**o**me | bionde_e cr**e**spe
  —F. Petrarca

  Penetrad sin tem**or**,| memorias m**í**as
  —L. de Góngora

He hath brought many captives | home to Rome
—W. Shakespeare

The two types are usually freely mixed; exceptions in which only one type is used, or both are set in purposeful patterns, do exist, but do not concern such a general treatise as this one.

Common trespassing to this structure include omitting the caesura, or stressing both the fourth and the sixth syllable: in the latter case there is usually some reason, phonetic or otherwise that highlights either syllable clearly.

The endecasillabo has played a major role in classic poetry: the Spanish symbolists loved it, the majority Italian poems from Dante to Montale uses this metre exclusively; Shakespeare freely mixes it with iambic pentameters in order to spice blank verse up, as may the diffident Reader may verify in his sonnet CLIII (actually some lines of it, e.g., number 4, can be read in both ways):

> Cupid laid by his brand and fell asleep:
> A maid of Dian's this advantage found,
> And his love-kindling fire did quickly steep
> In a cold valley-fountain of that ground;
> Which borrowed from this holy fire of Love,
> A dateless lively heat, still to endure,
> And grew a seething bath, which yet men prove
> Against strange maladies a sovereign cure.
> But at my mistress' eye Love's brand new-fired,
> The boy for trial needs would touch my breast;
> I, sick withal, the help of bath desired,
> And thither hied, a sad distempered guest,
> But found no cure, the bath for my help lies
> Where Cupid got new fire; my mistress' eyes.

(Probably one of the works the Magnanimous Shade of the Bard would like to have buried with himself).

Gallic Decasyllable

Proper endecasillabi are terribly rare in French (Guillaume de Machaut, to name somebody famous, uses something similar, at times); however, one of the most common verse types in France is very similar to the endecasillabo, of which it can well be considered a simplified form. This verse is the Gallic decasyllable, which has two mandatory stresses, one on the fourth and one on the tenth syllable. The first occurrences of this verse are lost in the haze of time: it was used by Raimbaut de Vaqueiras in his epic letter, one of the extremely rare examples of long poems in troubadouric literature; in Northern France it was certainly already very widespread during the second half of the XIV century, when Jean Froissart and Deschampes used it extensively; popular during the Pléiade age, it culminated with Valéry, who employed it in his longest masterpiece, 'Le Cimetière marin'. This verse is called 'Gallic' in this guide to account for both its Provençal origin and its presence in France, not simply to pester the Reader with a rare adjective. Here are two examples, one for each language and both from the same period, the late twelfth century:

> Valen marqu**es**, senher de Monferr**at**,
> a Dieu graz**i**sc quar vos a tant onr**at**
> > —Raimbaut de Vaqueiras

> Au renovi**au** de la douçor d'est**é**
> Que resclarc**i**st la doix en la font**ai**ne
> > —Gace Brulé

However, it is to be noted that no verse ever dominated French poetry at any point the way the endecasillabo does Italian: the mediaeval octasyllable was never really abandoned, experimentation was ever present and, oftentimes, sharp caesuras were used to break long verses, rather than introducing internal constraints on stresses. There is, however, a multipurpose verse in that language, and it is called *alexandrine*.

Alexandrine

The alexandrine is often defined as an iambic hexameter with a caesura after the third foot, a definition that covers only part of the possible cases (in two words, mild bull). In the actual classic tradition, this verse line is formed by adjoining two verses of six metrical syllables each; in French the first one is almost always masculine, so that the alexandrine can be practically defined as a line of twelve metrical syllables with a stress on the sixth and a caesura immediately after it.

This metre does not quite dominate French poetry like the endecasillabo does Italian, but it is by far the most used nonetheless, with so many examples a good one is found (at last) without even sweating:

ANGOISSE

Je ne viens pas ce s**oi**r | vaincre ton corps, ô b**ê**te
En qui vont les péch**és** | d'un peuple, ni creus**er**
Dans tes cheveux imp**urs** | une triste temp**ê**te
Sous l'incurable enn**ui** | que verse mon baisi**er**:

Je demande_à ton l**it** | le lourd sommeil sans s**o**nges
Planant sous les rid**eaux** | inconnus du rem**o**rds,
Et que tu peux goût**er** | après tes noires mens**o**nges
Toi qui sur le né**a**nt | en sait plus que les m**o**rts.

Car le Vice, ronge**a**nt | ma native nobl**e**sse
M'a comme toi marqu**é** | de sa stérilit**é**,
Mais tandis que ton s**ei**n | de pierre est habit**é**

Par un coeur que la d**e**nt | d'aucun crime ne bl**e**sse,
Je fuis pâle, déf**ai**t, | hanté par mon linc**eu**l,
Ayant peur de mour**i**r | lorsque je couche s**eu**l.
　　　　　　　　　　—S. Mallarmé

I don't come tonight to win your body, O beast
in which the sins of a population gather, nor to stir,
within your impure hair, a mournful tempest
by the helpless ennui my kiss pours:

I ask your bed for heavy slumber, unaffected by dreams
that slither from under the curtains, unknown by the remorse,
[slumber] one can savour after your black lies,
you who know, about nothing, more than the dead do.

Since vice, gnawing on my native nobility
Has branded both of us with its sterility,
But as long as your stony breast is haunted

By a heart the fangs of no crime can wound
I flee, pale, undone, hounded by my bed sheet,
Fearing to die if I sleep alone.

Alexandrines do exist in Spanish, and usually have thirteen metrical syllables:

En el nomne glori**o**so | del Rey omnipot**e**nt
　　　　　　—Gonzalo de Berceo

Rumour has the alexandrine was introduced for the first time in the *Roman d'Alexandre*, a fifteenth-century French novel, and that it was hardly ever used in Italy. However, by comparing the French variety, in which the first hemistich is masculine, and the Spanish variety, in which it is feminine, it is legitimate to wonder whether a hemistich with a triple ending was ever devised. The answer is in the affirmative: it happened in Sicily in the early thirteenth century, thus long predating the French 'invention': again we have a verse with a caesura preceded and followed by hemistichs with six metrical syllables each. Here is a very typical (and quite famous) example by Cielo d'Alcamo:

Rosa fresca_aulent**i**ssima | ch'apari_inver l'est**a**te
le donne ti dis**i**ano, | pulzell'e marit**a**te
tràgemi d'este f**o**cora, | se t'este a bolont**a**te

The Italian alexandrine, therefore, typically has fourteen metrical syllables; one ought to consider, however, that the charm of this metre has much to do with its ambiguous nature, with it being one and two verses at one time; the nature of its hemistichs is then, perhaps, the most relevant feature the ear of the reader catches.

One drawback of the Hundred Years' War is that alexandrines are extremely rare, though easy to write, in English. G. M. Hopkins sometimes uses the iambic hexameter, whose variety often overlaps that of the alexandrine, but the most famous exception to this ban is found in Edmund Spenser who, being already busy enough hating the Spanish and Italian, thought he could afford the risk of placing a single specimen of this horribly French line under the weight of eight patriotic iambic pentameters. His alexandrines are almost invariably actual iambic hexameters, with few exceptions like this one:

And therefore wisht me st**ay** | till I more truth should find

Iambic Pentameter

We have seen that classic English poetry may use several metres; however, like other languages, it favours one kind above all: since the fourteenth century this kind is the iambic pentameter. This verse is usually defined, as the name suggests, as a sequence of five iambs; most prosody treatises stop here in the definition, while others, proving their authors have at least read some Shakespeare and/or Marlowe, realise that some of the 'iambic feet' do not actually carry any accent, and introduce wispy concepts as 'virtual' or 'possible' stresses. Further readings teach these enlightened colleagues of ours that a number of these verses actually end with an amphibrach, and so introduce the idea of 'feminine iambic pentameter', making quite a mess of the whole matter.

Examples of both the 'exceptions' mentioned are easily found through all the iambic pentameter works of Shakespeare, e.g., in the beginning of son-net CII

> My love is strengthened, though more weak in **see**ming;
> I love not less, though less the show appear;
> That love is merchandized, whose rich est**ee**ming,

while iambic pentameters carrying less than five stresses are very common in both Marlowe and Shelley, e.g.:

> The tr**u**mpet of a pr**o**phecy! O w**i**nd

It is quite obvious to the Reader, one would hope, that all these nags in the definition of this most popular English verse could be removed by adopting a definition in line with those adopted for the endecasillabo and the alexan-drine: *the iambic pentameter is a verse of ten metrical syllables which carries no stresses on odd-positioned (first, third, seventh, etc.) syllables.*

People educated in Anglo-Saxon countries usually react very strongly against this concept, for different reasons (the references will unearth some of them to you), and it is therefore worth considering the matter more in depth. Even those few obdurate enough to stress the 'of' and the 'y' in 'prophecy' in the Shelley line above would have a hard time applying the same policy throughout Marlowe's translation of Ovid's Elegy VII (book II):

> The parrot, from east India to me sent
> Is dead; all fowls her exequies frequent
> Go, godly birds, striking your breasts bewail,
> And with rough claws your tender cheeks assail

Strictly following the iambic pentameter idea in this case would force the reader to stress 'from' and 'to' in the first line, whereas both are words no sane English speaker would highlight. The third line is entirely off the pat-tern, but it is interesting to notice how *in all of Marlowe's poetic work there is no single line that has more, or less, than ten exact metrical syllables.* The same is valid for Shakespeare's sonnets and for a number of other Elizabethan poets, making it a general rule that the foreign criterion of counting syllables was felt much more strongly than the national one of arraying feet.

And now, the most hidden secret of English poetry being revealed, you can, kind Reader, proceed to the next chapter with a light heart.

Sources and further reading

Only very specialistic books discuss versification without treating also rhyming and poetic forms; the text mentioned here should therefore be thought of as valid readings for anybody interested in the subjects the next three chapters treat as well, and they will not be repeated there. Among these general treatises are, as far as English is concerned, Attridge, D. *Poetic Rhythm: An Introduction* (Cambridge: Cambridge University Press, 1995), Saintsbury, G. *History of English Prosody* (London: Macmillan and Co., 1910), Thompson, J. *The Founding of English Metre.* (London : Routledge & K. Paul, 1961) and, above all, the mother of all meta-texts, namely, Brogan, T. V. F. *English Versification 1570–1980. A Reference Guide With a Global Appendix* (Baltimore: Johns Hopkins University Press, 1981), which contains a list of references that stretch as far as Mongolian poetry.

For Italian, the subject is less controversial, and the worst one can find in a book is incompleteness or excessive verbosity; fairly good texts are Del Monte, A. *Retorica, stilistica e versificazione* (Torino: Loescher, 1981), Elwert, W. Th. *Versificazione italiana dalle origini ai nostri giorni* (Firenze: Le Monnier, 1976). Fubini, M. *Metrica e poesia. Lezioni sulle forme metriche italiane* (Milano: Feltrinelli, 1975) is monumental and perhaps the most complete, precious for following a strictly chronological criterion, while Ramous, M. *La metrica* (Milano: Garzanti, 1984) is probably the right thing to seek if one is just looking for an easy, quick overview.

French prosody treatises suffer from a good deal of chauvinism; Romains, J., and Chennevière, G. *Petit Traité de versification française* has been reprinted an amazing number of times, while the somewhat misinformed Morier (see the bibliography in chapter 7) enjoys a large popularity as well. Ruwet, N. *Langage, musique, poésie* (Paris: Editions du Seuil, 1972) approaches the matter somewhat more sensibly.

Spanish prosody is tricky, as it appears to be much simpler than it actually is; the Reader can refer to Bensoussan, A.; Bensoussan, M.; and Le Bigot, C. *Versification espagnole suivi de petit traite des figures* (Presses universitaires de Rennes, 1993), Baehr R., *Manual de versificacion española* (Madrid: Gredos, 1997), De Riquer, M. *Resumen de versificacion espanola* (Barcelona: Seix y Barral, 1950) and most of all to the extensive Navarro Tomas, T. *Metrica española* (2nd ed., Barcelona: Labor, 1995) to understand why; in particular, concepts of free verse that in the rest of Europe would appear only in the twentieth century were already well established in Spain by the seventeenth and how old Spanish seems to have been stress-timed. These concepts, and the related references, will be treated in later parts of this book.

To conclude, the relationship between music and verse in classical music (or at least in one of its most popular forms) is described in Lippmann, F. *Versificazione italiana e ritmo musicale: i rapporti tra verso e musica nell'opera italiana dell'Ottocento* (Napoli: Liguori, 1986).

II. Rhyming

Definition

A thing often assumed in vain to be known, rhyme is the perfect coincidence of all the sounds from the [last] stress of two words to their end. In Romance languages the statement has exactly the same meaning with or without the term 'last'; however, due to the existence in English of secondary stresses, it does make a difference here: e.g., 'circulate' carries a secondary stress on the a, whereas the primary one lies on the i, so that it could or could not be considered to rhyme with 'fate', according to whichever definition we are pleased to pick. Classic English poetry has systematically embraced the easier way, and assumes the two words do rhyme. This example by Shakespeare (from Sonnet XXXVIII) contains a similar example:

> Be thou the tenth muse, ten times more in worth
> Than those old nine which rhymers **invoc**ate
> And he that calls on thee, let him bring forth
> Eternal numbers to outlive long d**ate**

Of course, by referring to a poem as 'rhyming', prosody, as well as the layman, means that the last words of two (or more) verses are connected by rhyme; the occurrence of rhymes in the middle of verses will be covered in the chapter devoted to advanced poetic devices.

Rich Rhyme

Rich rhyme is a backward extension of ordinary rhyme. In less abstruse terms, this means the two sequences of sounds in the words start being matched before the last stressed vowel. Of course a rich rhyme is also an ordinary rime, and equally of course the vice-versa is not necessarily true. Rich rhyming isn't any popular in English; it is, and very much so, in decadent French poetry, where it is very much the rule rather than the exception, as is shown in this deliciously obscure sonnet, El Desdichado (the wretched) by Nerval:

Je suis le ténébreux,—le veuf,—l'inconsol**é**,
Le prince d'Aquitaine à la tour ab**olie**:
Ma seule étoile est morte,—et mon luth conste**llé**
Porte le soleil noir de la Mélanc**olie**.

Dans la nuit du tombeau, toi qui m'as consolé,
Rends-moi le Pausilippe et la mer d'Italie,
La fleur qui plaisait tant à mon coeur désolé
Et la treille où le pampre à la rose s'allie.

Suis-je Amour ou Phébus?... Lusignan ou Biron?
Mon front est rouge encor du baiser de la reine;
J'ai rêvé dans la grotte où nage la sirène...

Et j'ai deux fois vainqueur traversé l'Achéron:
Modulant tour à tour sur la lyre d'Orphée
Les soupirs de la sainte et les cris de la fée

I am the tenebrous, the widower, the unconsoled,
the Prince of Aquitaine by the forbidden tower:
my only star is dead and my spangled lute
carries the black sun of melancholy.

In the night of the tomb, you who have consoled me,
give me back Posilippo and the Italian sea,
the flower that my grieved heart liked so much
and the arbour where the vine and the rose are conjoined.

Am I Love or Phoebus?...Lusignan or Byron?
My brow still blushes from the kisses of the queen;
I have dreamt in the cave where the siren swims...

And I have crossed twice the Acheron as a conqueror:
modulating on Orpheus' lyre, as I went by,
the sighs of the saint and the fairy's cry.

Mirror Rhyme

An even more perverted form of rich rhyme, mirror rhyme is an extremely rare device, in which a word *phonetically* includes the other one entirely: for example there is mirror rhyme between 'cart' and 'art', 'clerk' and 'lark', 'flower' and 'hour' (the last being perhaps the most perused rhyming words in all Victorian England). To the knowledge of the present writer, there are no major examples of mirror riming in classic English poetry, although the very beginning of Keats' *Endymion* seems to contain more mirror couplets than statistics would account for; it was used extensively in a piece by Raimon de Miravalh, 'Aissi'm te amors franc' ('this way love keeps me fair'), and other Provençal troubadours used it from time to time, and never by mischance, as may be seen in this fragment of Bernart de Ventadorn's most famous song, 'Quan vei la lauzeta mover' ('when I see the meadowlark move'):

> Per la dousour que al cor li **vai**
> **Ai**!
> Quan gran enveja men ve

> .　　.　　.　　.

where a remarkable echo effect is achieved. However, by far the most systematic use of this device is found in Jean Renard's *Lai de l'ombre* ('lai of the mirror image'), a poem in octasyllabic couplets written around 1220 A.D. Here is its very beginning; keep in mind that two words that sound exactly the same (see next paragraph) qualify for mirror rhyme as well:

> Ne me vueil pas desaüser
> de bien dire, ançois vueil user
> mon sens a el qu'a estre oiseus.
> Je ne vueil pas resambler ceus
> qui sont garçon por tout destruire,
> quar, puis que j'ai le sens d'estruire
> aucun bien en dit ou en fet,
> vilains est qui ses gas en fet,
> se ma cortoisie s'aoevre
> a fere aucune plesant oevre
> ou il n'ait ramposne ne lait.

> .　　.　　.　　.　　.

Identity Rhyme

Identity rhyme is simply the phonetic identity of two words. They can have the same spelling as well, but it is not required: for example, 'bat' as an animal and 'bat' as a club is an acceptable couple, as is 'all' and 'awl' or 'talk' and 'torque' and so forth. In poetry, this sort of rhyme is often obtained by *combination* of two words, as in 'thinking' and 'th'inking'; Petrarca fairly often irks his readers with the 'l'aura' (th'air) 'Laura' (his mistress) match.

This device is often called 'rime riche' by Anglo-Saxon prosodists who, however, usually make quite a mess of its definition.

As identity rhyme conveys an idea of stillness bordering on obsession, its main use is in sextains, and examples of it are to be sought there (see Chapter V); occasionally, however, examples of it are found in simple couplets: in Racine's *Phèdre*, the protagonist, tormented by incestuous love for her stepson, says about him:

> Tu vois depuis quel temps il évite nos pas,
> Et cherche tous les lieux où nous ne sommes pas.
> —lines 621–622

Likewise, the chorus in Eliot's *Murder in the Cathedral* often refers to the immobility of destiny by this couplet:

> That the wheel may turn and still
> be forever still

Entire poems written in identity rhymes exist in archaic Italian poetry. The most notorious (and perhaps most successful) example is Guittone d'Arezzo's 'Tuttor, s'eo veglio o dormo', an amazing work composed of 36 ambiguous couplets, which are far more difficult to contrive in Italian than they are in French or English:

> Tuttor, s'eo veglio o dormo,
> di lei pensar non campo,
> ch' Amor en cor m'atacca.
> E tal voler ho d'òr mo,
> com' di sappar in campo
> o di creder a tacca.
> E bon sapemi, como
> eo n'acquistasse Como;
> ma' che diritto n'ò,
> perch'eo non dico no
> di lei servir mai dì,
> dica chi vol: 'Maidì!'

Bon ho diritto 'n somma
s'en amar lei m'aduco
del cor tutt'e dell'alma,
perch'è di valor somma;
e che piacer aduco,
dat'a amor dell'alma
che più m'ama che sé!
Ciò dia saver, che, se
torn'a suo pregio magno,
per me onta no magn'ò,
ché, si ben m'am'a dobbio,
m'è al certo che dobbio.

Om ch' ama pregio e pò,
più che legger en scola,
Amor valeli pro:
ché più leggero è Po
a passar senza scola
che lo mondo a om pro'
senza Amor, che dà
cor e bisogno da
sprovar valor e forzo;
perché ciascun om, for zo
che briga e travagli' agia,
se vale, non varrà già.

Amor già per la gioia
che 'nde vegna non laudo,
quanto per lo travaglio
ch'e per aver la gioia
ch'è tal, sua par non l'audo.
Ver' che varria, travaglio,
s'eo la teness'ad agio
ben sempre a meo agio:
poi tutte gioie l'om'à,
varrea, non val oma';
fallo grand'agio vile,
per che tal gioi' mal vil'e.

Poso e travaglio mésto,
dato e tolto a modo,
sempre piacere è me,
e de ciascuno me sto
sì bonamente a modo,
gran pagamento è me.
E val, sembrami, meglio,
quanto riso ver' méglio,
sperar ch'aver d'amica:
ché, poi l'ama, né-mic'à
ver' che sperava averne,
e de gran state a vern'è.

Scuro saccio che par lo
mio detto, ma' che parlo
a chi s'entend' ed ame:
ché lo 'ngegno mio dàme
ch'i' me pur provi d'onne
mainera, e talento ònne.
Move, canzone, adessa,
vanne 'n Arezzo ad essa
da cui tegno ed ò,
se 'n alcun ben mi do;
e di' che presto so'
di tornar, se vol, so.

At any moment, be I awake or **asleep**
I don't **stop** *thinking of her,*
since love **binds** *my heart.*
And I have such a desire for **gold, at the moment**,
as I have of working in a **field**
or of lending money with a **token**.
Still, I like this, **as if**
I were to win **Como**;
what right do **I have**,
since I never say **no**
to serve her, **ever**,
say who wants, **"so help me God!"**

*I have a valid right, **in the end**,*
*if **I put**, in loving her,*
*all my heart and **soul**,*
*because she's the **peak** of worth;*
*and what a pleasure **I get**,*
*given to the love of the **soul***
*that loves me more than **herself**!*
*She must know that **if***
*this is **eminently** good on her part,*
*there is no **greater** shame for me,*
*because, if she loves me well, **twice** as much*
*I certainly **should** love her.*

*A man that loves worth **can**,*
*more than from a lesson in **school**,*
*profit **much** from Love:*
*it is easier to pass the **Po***
*without a **barge***
*than for a **brave** man [to walk on] this world*
*without Love, that **gives***
*heart and need **to***
*put valiance and **strength** to the test;*
*since each man, **without having***
*first **being tried**, through care and labour,*
*for his worth, is**n't** worth **anything**.*

*It isn't quite for the **joy***
*that comes of it that **I praise** Love:*
*it is for the **labour***
that one undergoes in order to have [that] joy.
*Which is greater than anything **I've** ever **heard of***
***I am worth much more** than I would be*
*if I had her, **easily**,*
*always **at my disposal**:*
*when **a man has** all joy,*
*he is not worth **all that** he'd be otherwise, no matter how*
much that is;
*great leisure be**little**s him,*
*while hardly the joys of love are **small**.*

*Peace **mixed** with labour,*
***periodical**ly given and taken away,*
***is** always a pleasure **for me**,*
*and both **leave me***
*so perfectly **balanced***
*that it is a great satisfaction **for me**.*
*And it is, it seems to me, **better***
*(the same way rice is better than **millet**)*
*to hope for than to have a **lover**:*
*since, once one has love, he **doesn't quite** get,*
*in fact, what he was hoping **for***
*and from a warm Summer he falls into **Winter**.*

*I know **one thinks** it is unclear*
what** I say, but I am **speaking
*for those who understand and **love**:*
*my wit **makes it so** that*
*I test myself in **every***
*way and **I** intend **to do it**.*

*Get away, **now**, song,*
*go to Arezzo, **to her***
*from which **I have** and keep*
*every good thing **I** happen to **meet**;*
*and tell her that **I can***
*become **hers** again, if she wants.*

Virtual Rhyme

This is a false rhyme that exists only in English and is strictly connected to the nature of iambic verse: since an ideal reader would stress all even syllables (see chapter I), lines are assumed to rime when their last even syllables (in a pentameter, the tenth ones), and whatever comes after, are matched. This excerpt from Shakespeare's sonnet CV falls in such case, at least for a contemporary reader:

Let not my love be call'd id**o**latr**y**,
Nor my beloved as an idol show,
Since all alike my songs and praises b**e**
To one, of one, still such, and ever so.

As one can see, the élan of the iambic versification is supposed, in this case, to shift the weight of one's attention and intonation on the Y rather than on the O in 'idolatry', making it rhyme with 'be' and resetting the number of metrical syllables to a regular ten.

It goes without saying that Continental readers regard this device as insipid, if not entirely pointless, perhaps because they are not used to it. Perhaps.

Assonance and Consonance

We have stated in the beginning that rhyme is a relationship that connects two words through the perfect coincidence of each sound from the last stressed vowel onward. When, instead of *all* the sounds, only the consonants are matched, the relationship is called *consonance*, whereas if only the vowels are matched, it is called *assonance*. These two terms are also, sometimes, used to denote identity of *all* consonantal (or vocalic, respectively) sounds in two words, regardless of where the stress falls. The practice is never followed in the present treatise, but the Reader should be warned about it, lest he be rather confused when reading other sources.

Assonance and consonance are often used by inconsiderate scribblers to substitute for rhyme proper; no examples of that, however, will be shown, for two excellent reasons: the first being that they are little agreeable, the second that all those the Present Author can think of are still under copyright.

More decent poets use these devices for diverse purposes, such as linking different groups of rhymes, or in specifically devised forms. Assonance, for example, is the foundation of several Spanish forms, and it is the ground upon which the Spanish symbolists have tailored their free verse. In most poems of this current, the same assonance is used every other line, throughout the whole work (the effect is underlined more by the fact that, usually, feminine words are employed for this). An example by Antonio Machado:

> Me dijo un'alba de la primavera:
> Yo florecí en tu corazón sombrío
> ha muchos años, caminante viejo
> que no cortes las flores del camino.

Tu corazón de sombra ¿acaso guarda
el viejo aroma de mis viejos lirios?
¿Perfuman aún mis rosas de la albe frente
del hada de tu sueno adamantino?

Respondí a la mañana:
Sólo tienen cristal los sueños mios.
Yo no conozco el hada de mis sueños;
ni sé si está mi corazon florido.

Pero si aguardas la mañana pura
que ha da romper el vaso cristalino,
quizás el hada te dará tus rosas,
mi corazón tus lirios.

A Springtime dawn told me:
I flourished in your sombre heart
many years ago, wandering old man
that do not cut the flowers on the road.

Does your shadowy heart treasure
the old smell of my old lilies?
Do my roses perfume the pale brow
of the fairy of your adamantine dream?

I answered the morning:
my dreams have only crystals.
I don't know the fairy of my dreams;
nor do I know whether my heart is blooming.

But if you await the pure morning
that has to break the crystal vase,
perhaps the fairy will give you your roses,
[and] my heart your lilies.

Consonance, at least partial, is more common than assonance in English, where vowels are such a mess, but it is not usually employed in such a systematic way. S. T. Coleridge who, unfortunately, lacked the help and comfort of the present guide, and had therefore misunderstood almost everything about alliterative verse (see chapter VII), often uses it to conjoin the hemistichs of the unrhymed lines in *The Rime of the Ancient Mariner*:

The sun now rose upon the right:
out of the sea came he,
still hid in mist, and on the left
went down into the sea.

Sources and further reading

As hinted before, the same bibliography provided in the previous chapter will do for this one as well; Jean Renard's *Lai de l'ombre* is one of the most celebrated examples of a refined use of rhymes, and several essays and articles have been written on the subject; among those, Cooper, L.F. *Romance Philology*, 35 (1981–82): 250 is concerned with the topic of literary reflectiveness.

III. Closed Forms

Verse Forms

We shall divide verse forms into two groups; the first one we shall treat, *closed* forms, includes those that have a fixed number of stanzas and lines, or one that varies within a very narrow range. Some of these forms, such as the sonnet, were fashionable once and a few, such as the haiku, still are but, given the general difficulty in using them, and the general incompetence of modern poets, most of these schemes are thoroughly obsolete. They are, however, clear archetype, and that is why it is worth treating some of them in full detail.

Sonnet

Absolutely the most common and abused form of all, the sonnet has been plaguing Italian poetry since the thirteenth century, and has rapidly invaded, with little variations, all Europe. The sonnet uniquely fits corny themes, as its fourteen lines allow the writer to be bombastic, but fall just short of letting him realise he's making a fool of himself. In spite of that, the form has been so popular that thousands of good sonnets exist, and several great ones as well. None of them, of course, deals with love.

We owe to the Baroque age the discovery that sonnets could be employed for something kinder than sticking stars in the eyes of the poet's mistress; Baroque poets thought them more fit for describing whipped beauties, flies drowning in an inkwell and, most of all, clockworks. Although clocks still enjoyed some popularity during symbolism, Baudelaire and his mates found the form to apply more to chasms, storms, albatrosses, statues and corpses. This movement is perhaps the one that produced the best sonnets: an example of this is the piece by Mallarmé shown in chapter two; a baroque example, instead, is this by L. de Góngora:

DE UNA DAMA QUE, QUITÁNDOSE UNA SORTIJA, SE PICÓ CON UN ALFILER

Prisión del nácar era articulado
(de mi firmeza un émulo luciente)
un dïamante, ingenïosamente
en oro también él aprisionado.

Clori, pues, que su dedo apremïado
de metal, aun precioso, no consiente,
gallarda un día, sobre impacïente,
lo redimió del vínculo dorado.

Mas, ay, que insidïoso latón breve
en los cristales de su bella mano
sacrílego divina sangre bebe:

púrpura ilustró menos indïano
marfil; invidïosa, sobre nieve
claveles deshojó la Aurora en vano.

OF A LADY WHO, TAKING OFF A RING, PRICKED HERSELF WITH A PIN

A prison for set nacre
(a shining imitator of my own firmness)
a diamond, ingeniously,
was imprisoned as well.

Chloris, who won't have her finger
by metal, no matter how precious, oppressed,
one day, graceful and overly impatient,
relieved it of its golden bond.

But, alas! an insidious sliver of brass,
among the crystals of her dainty hand,
gloats on blood divine:

Purple didn't blaze as much on Indian
ivory; envious, on the snow,
Dawn shed its carnations in vain.

Technically speaking, all sonnets are made of 14 verses; many find it pleasant to split them in two quatrains and two tercets. The matrix on which they are formed is the *Petrarchan sonnet* called so (but in English only) because it was invented a good fifty years before Petrarca's birth, and in consideration of the fact that this quite tedious Great used it without introducing anything new in its development.

The rhymes for the first eight verses, with the usual conventions, may be either ABAB ABAB or ABBA ABBA, followed by any permutation of six verses (e.g., CDE EDC or CDC CDC), whose only constraint is that each of them must rhyme with at least one other. The shortest possible example, *Sur la femme* by Charles Cros is here provided:

Ô
Femme,
Flamme,
Eau!

Au
Drame
L'âme
Faut.

Même
Qui
L'aime

S'y
Livre
Ivre.

O woman, flame, water!
Soul suits drama.
Even those who love it
Float there drunk.

The rime scheme here is the rather common ABBA ABBA CDC DEE.

Evidence that the Petrarchan sonnet preceded the birth of Francesco Petrarca (whichever barbarous spelling of his name one might choose to adopt), esq., of Arezzo, Italy, by over fifty years, can be easily gathered. One piece of it among hundreds, by Giacomo da Lentini (first half of the thirteenth century) can be enjoyed here:

A l'aire scuro ho vista ploggia dare,
ed a lo scuro rendere clarore;
e a foco arzente ghiaccia diventare
e freda neve rendere calore.

E dolze cose molto amareare,
e de l'amare rendere dolzore;
e dui guerrieri in fina pace stare
e 'ntra dui amici nascereci errore.

Ed ho vista d'Amor cosa più forte:
ch'era feruto e sanòmi ferendo;
lo foco donde ardea stutò con foco.

La vita che mi dè fue la mia morte;
lo foco che mi strinse, ora ne 'ncendo:
ché sì mi trasse Amor, non trovo loco.

I have seen a bright sky giving rain
and a dark one give clarity back
and [I've seen] a soaring fire turn to ice
and cold snow yield heat

and sweet things turn bitter
and bitter ones yield sweetness;
and two warriors sit in peace
and discord arise between two friends.

And I've seen from Love something more outlandish:
since I was wounded, and wounding me he healed me;
he smothered with fire the fire that was burning me.

The life it gave me was my death;
the fire it quenched now burns me:
Since love drags me thus, I find no rest.

Italian sonnets are almost invariably written in endecasillabi, and several Spanish ones (as seen above) are as well. French sonnets, which may follow the same rules concerning rhymes, or follow the English ones (see below), are commonly written in alexandrines. Of course, as Cros demonstrated with his monosyllables, just any verse can be employed as well. This is generally true for all open and closed forms, with few exceptions, concentrated mostly in Italian poetry.

Petrarchan sonnets have been written in English: the most notorious ones are by Donne and Milton; the latter wrote this:

> How soon hath Time, the subtle thief of youth,
> Stol'n on his wing my three-and-twentieth year!
> My hasting days fly on with full career,
> But my late spring no bud or blossom shew'th.
>
> Perhaps my semblance might deceive the truth
> That I to manhood am arriv'd so near;
> And inward ripeness doth much less appear,
> That some more timely-happy spirits endu'th.
>
> Yet it be less or more, or soon or slow,
> It shall be still in strictest measure ev'n
> To that same lot, however mean or high,
>
> Toward which Time leads me, and the will of Heav'n:
> All is, if I have grace to use it so
> As ever in my great Task-Master's eye.

However, given the difficulty of finding so many rhymes in English or, if you want, due to the fact poets in English hate to toil too much, they soon transformed the sonnet into something in which the rhyme-sets of the two opening quatrains differ from each other, and the two tercets end in a couplet.

Thus the English sonnet has, typically, a ABAB CDCD EFE FDD rhyme scheme, just as Shakespeare's sonnet CXXXVII:

> Thou blind fool, Love, what dost thou to mine eyes,
> That they behold, and see not what they see?
> They know what beauty is, see where it lies,
> Yet what the best is take the worst to be.
>
> If eyes, corrupt by over-partial looks,
> Be anchored in the bay where all men ride,
> Why of eyes' falsehood hast thou forged hooks,
> Whereto the judgment of my heart is tied?
>
> Why should my heart think that a several plot,
> Which my heart knows the wide world's common place?
> Or mine eyes, seeing this, say this is not,

To put fair truth upon so foul a face?
In things right true my heart and eyes have erred,
And to this false plague are they now transferred.

A compromise between the Italian and English form was attempted by Spenser who, in his *Amoretti*, tries on an ABAB BCBC CDC DEE rime scheme with some success but almost no followers at all.

Quatorzain

'Quatorzain' is a name collectively given to anamorphic or abortive sonnets, some of which, as Verlaine's *Nevermore*, are truly excellent. Their common characteristic is having 14 lines and something else in common with a sonnet, typically the fact of being split into two tercets and two quatrains. This form includes a pinnacle of English literature such as Shelley's *Ozymandias*, which sounds like an odd, customised patchwork of the English and Italian forms.

Limerick

The limerick is an absolutely British (although some have been written in other English-speaking countries, most notably in Ireland) and systematically humorous verse form. No 'serious' limerick is known, and few decent ones are. A limerick is formed of five verses rhymed AABBA; strictly speaking, the A-rhymed lines should be made of three amphibrachs each, and the B-rimed lines of two anapaests each.

Often all the lines are masculine and, as a consequence, the ending amphibrachs are lopped to iambs; this, however, greatly spoils the frisky rhythm of this verse.

Traditionally, the first line of a limerick ends with the name of a person or town.

An interesting selection of limericks was published in the mid 1800's by Edward Lear, and some acknowledge him as the inventor of the form; here is one:

There was an Old Man who supposed
The street door was partially closed;
But some very large rats,
Ate his coat and his hats,
While that futile old gentleman dozed.

Limericks are a relatively modern form, and exist, in their strictest version, in English only; however, they have been known to appear in Italian and French, in slightly modified versions.

Villanelle

The villanelle was, in mediaeval times, a popular form in Southern Italy and France, and as such it was snobbed for centuries by classic poets of those countries. It has become, however, quite popular in England ever since Queen Elizabeth's time, and it still is, there and overseas, featuring pieces from W. H. Auden and Dylan Thomas, for example. Outside French and English, the current version of this quite abstruse verse form is almost unknown (although Carlos Germán Belli has written one in Spanish, see below). It is interesting to notice that until Jean Passerat (late sixteenth century) wrote his bit, it was simply an open form with two rhymes and repeated lines, and therefore merely a subtype of the virelai (see chapter V).

The villanelle is a true poet's nightmare: it is composed of five tercets followed by a quatrain, and it is based on two rhymes only, according to the scheme

ABA AB1 AB3 AB1 AB3 AB13

where the numbers indicate that, instead of creating a new line, the one occupying that position must be repeated. The overall effect of a villanelle is therefore somewhat obsessive, as two of its 19 verses are repeated four times each. This explanation may not seem to be exceedingly clear, but the perversion of the form is perfectly apparent in these outstanding examples, of which the French one was the 'model' for the whole genre:

LLEVARTE quiero dentro de mi piel,
si bien en lontananza aún te acecho,
para rescatar la perdida miel.

Contemplándote como un perro fiel,
en el día te sigo trecho a trecho,
que haberte quiero dentro de mi piel.

No más el sabor de la cruda hiel,
y en paz quedar conmigo y ya rehecho,
rescatando así la perdida miel.

Ni viva aurora, ni oro, ni clavel,
y en cambio por primera vez el hecho
de llevarte yo dentro de mi piel.

Verte de lejos no es asunto cruel,
sino el raro camino que me he hecho,
para rescatar la perdida miel.

El ojo mío nunca te es infiel,
aun estando distante de tu pecho,
que haberte quiero dentro de mi piel,
y así rescatar la perdida miel.
                                        —Carlos German Belli

I want to carry you inside my skin,
albeit I still observe you from afar,
to make up for the lost honey.

Contemplating you as a faithful hound,
by day I follow you step by step,
since I want to carry you inside my skin.

No more the taste of the crude bitterness,
and again being at peace with myself,
thus making up for the lost honey.

Neither lively dawn, nor gold nor carnation,
and, instead, for the first time, the fact
of carrying you inside my skin.

Seeing you from afar in not quite a cruel thing,
instead, it is the odd path I have made for myself,
to make up for the lost honey.

To you my eye isn't ever unfaithful,
though being far from your breast,
since I want to carry you inside my skin
to make up for the lost honey.

THEOCRITUS

O Singer of Persephone!
In the dim meadows desolate
Dost thou remember Sicily?

Still through the ivy flits the bee
Where Amaryllis lies in state;
O Singer of Persephone!

Simætha calls on Hecate
And hears the wild dogs at the gate;
Dost thou remember Sicily?

Still by the light and laughing sea
Poor Polypheme bemoans his fate:
O Singer of Persephone!

And still in boyish rivalry
Young Daphnis challenges his mate:
Dost thou remember Sicily?

Slim Lacon keeps a goat for thee,
For thee the jocund shepherds wait,
O Singer of Persephone!
Dost thou remember Sicily?

—Oscar Wilde

J'AI perdu ma tourterelle;
Est-ce point celle que j'oy?
Je veux aller après elle.

Tu regrettes ta femelle,
Hélas! aussi fais-je moy.
J'ai perdu ma tourterelle.

Si ton amour est fidelle,
Aussi est ferme ma foy;
Je veux aller après elle.

Ta plainte se renouvelle,
Toujours plaindre je me doy;
J'ai perdu ma tourterelle.

En ne voyant plus la belle,
Plus rien de beau je ne voy;
Je veux aller après elle.

Mort, que tant de fois j'appelle,
Prends ce qui se donne à toy!
J'ai perdu ma tourterelle;
Je veux aller après elle.

—Jean Passerat

I have lost my turtle-dove;
Is it her I am hearing?
I want to go after her.

You miss your female,
Alas! So do I:
I have lost my turtle-dove.

If your love is constant,
So is the firmness of my faithfulness:
I want to go after her.

You renew your complaint,
I should complain all the time:
I have lost my turtle-dove.

Since I no longer see that beauty
I no longer see anything beautiful;
I want to go after her.

Death, whom so many times I call for,
Take the one that gives himself to you!
I have lost my turtle-dove:
I want to go after her.

Villanelles don't seem to fit a single genre, and have been used for any kind of poetry, mostly bad one.

Haiku

The haiku is a very common classic Japanese form that has recently been met with great popularity in the Western World, mostly on account of the fact that any fool can write a 17-syllables poem without excessive problems. That, of course, doesn't make a good haiku, a thing actually unknown to European languages.

Technically speaking, a haiku is a poem of three lines, the second of which is made of seven syllables (actual, not metrical), and the other two of five syllables. They must contain a 'season word' (such as 'cherry blossom' for Springtime or 'still pond' for Summer) and a 'cutting word' (such as 'fall', 'dive'), and forbid similes and other such conceptual rhetoric, but are systematically laden, at least in their original language, with alliteration, assonance and word play. A rough example could be this one:

> Hawks on frosty boughs
> rhymesters incompetently
> write haiku under.

Worthy haiku deal with season themes and plenty of them exist (the rumour has) in Japanese, which the Present Author cannot read; in case the Reader is able to do so, we offer him this classic (romanised in the standard way):

> Tabi ni yande
> yume wa kareno o
> kakemeguru

> —Basho

This form has been used in Japanese, English and French at the least.

Quatrain

This name covers a heterogeneous group of rhymed poems of four verses of the same type. Generally, they all carry the same rhyme, but they may also follow (in ascending order of rarity) ABAB, AABB or ABBA patterns; an excellent example of this form is the piece by Villon shown in the first chapter; an English one is Coleridge's *On Donne's Poetry*:

> With Donne, whose muse on dromedary trots,
> Wreathe iron pokers into true-love knots;
> Rhyme's sturdy cripple, fancy's maze and clue,
> Wit's forge and fire-blast, meaning's press and screw.

This metre doesn't seem to particularly fit a specific mood but, due to its brevity, it hardly adapts to lyricism.

Quatrains are extremely common in French, since the earliest middle-ages, fairly so in English, unusual in Italian, sporadic in Spanish and extremely rare in Provençal.

Cinquain

This is an ambiguous term, covering two separate forms, one decent, classic, French and mediaeval, the other newfangled and American.

The first form is based on two riming groups, arranged at will over five verses of the same type. It was rediscovered and largely employed by Apollinaire in his *Bestiaire*, to which belongs this piece titled 'Le Serpent' ('the snake'):

> Tu t'acharnes sur la beauté.
> Et quelles femmes ont été
> Victimes de ta cruauté!
> Ève, Euridice, Cléopâtre ;
> J'en connais encor trois ou quatre.

> *You torment beauty.*
> *And, oh the women who have been*
> *subject to your cruelty!*
> *Eve, Eurydice, Cleopatra;*
> *I know three or four more.*

This type of cinquain is very close to the quatrain, and is an almost exclusively French form, doomed to stay so until a new generation of poets, enlightened by this guide, will realise that adding a line to a quatrain is somehow possible also in English. The *other* form of cinquain is a poem of five unrhymed lines, the first of which has two syllables, the second four, the third six, the fourth eight, and the last, again, two, as in:

My friend,
there's no saying
which sort of children games,
or choices of line breaks is verse
today.

People in the United States seem to love this form, but it is sometimes used in England as well, with equally horrid results.

Sextain

The sextain is likely the most difficult verse form ever devised; the first one, 'Lo ferm voler qu'el cor m'intra' was written by the Provençal troubadour Arnaut Daniel, in the middle of the twelfth century. Later, Dante who held Arnaut in great esteem wrote one as well ('Al poco giorno e al gran cerchio d'ombra') and Petrarca, who in turn longed to imitate Dante, wrote some dozens of them which no mortal up to today has yet managed to read in a row without falling asleep long ere the end was in sight.

Due to this masterpiece of tedium, the sextain is generally considered, in English-speaking countries, to have originated in Italy, and it has become customary, among those wishing to display a savoury international taste, to call it its Italian name, 'sestina'.

Technically speaking, a sextain is made of six stanzas of six verses each, followed by an envoi of three verses; each line belongs to one of six groups of *identity rhymes* (see chapter II) according to the scheme:

ABCDEF FAEBDC CFDABE ECBFAD DEACFB BDFECA ECA

It is also considered quite elegant to insert one word of each the B, D and F identity-rhyme groups inside the three verses of the envoi, but this is not systematically done, and actually several modern pieces don't even have an envoi.

Since finding six or seven words that sound exactly the same is almost impossible, repeating end-words is inevitable when writing a sextain, and this repetition gives the form its haunting character.

Since the renaissance, sextain have been spotted, though not too often, in English, while they are exceedingly rare in French; the most common usage of this metre is for poems dealing with love obsession, but even this is not systematically the case. The best-known English example the Present Author can think of is 'Altaforte' by Ezra Pound; a fairly famous Petrarchan example is 'Giovene donna sotto un verde lauro'; here is also an interesting piece by Kipling followed by Arnaut Daniel's holotype:

Giovene donna sotto un verde lauro
vidi, più bianca e più fredda che neve
non percossa dal sol molti e molt'anni;
e 'l suo parlare, e 'l bel viso, e le chiome
mi piacquen sì, ch'io l'ho dinanzi a gli occhi
ed avrò sempre, ov'io sia, in poggio o 'n riva.

Allora saranno i miei pensier a riva
che foglia verde non si trovi in lauro;
quando avrò queto il core, asciutti gli occhi,
vedrem ghiacciare il foco, arder la neve.
Non ho tanti capelli in queste chiome
quanti vorrei quel giorno attender anni.

Ma perché vola il tempo e fuggon gli anni,
sì ch'a la morte in un punto s'arriva,
o colle brune o colle bianche chiome,
seguirò l'ombra di quel dolce lauro,
per lo più ardente sole e per la neve,
fin che l'ultimo dì chiuda quest'occhi.

Non fûr già mai veduti sì begli occhi
o ne la nostra etade o ne' prim'anni,
che mi struggon così come 'l sol neve;
onde procede lagrimosa riva,
ch'Amor conduce a piè del duro lauro
c'ha i rami di diamante e d'òr le chiome.

I' temo di cangiar pria vólto e chiome
che con vera pietà mi mostri gli occhi
l'idolo mio scolpito in vivo lauro;
ché, s'al contar non erro, oggi ha sett'anni
che sospirando vo di riva in riva
la notte e 'l giorno, al caldo ed a la neve.

Dentro pur foco e fòr candida neve,
sol con questi pensier, con altre chiome,
sempre piangendo andrò per ogni riva,
per far forse pietà venir ne gli occhi
di tal che nascerà dopo mill'anni,
sé tanto viver po' ben cólto lauro.

L'auro e i topazii al sol sopra la neve
vincon le bionde chiome presso a gli occhi
che menan gli anni miei sì tosto a riva.
—Francesco Petrarca

A young woman under a green bay tree
I saw, whiter and colder than snow
unbeaten by the sun for many, many years;
and her speech, and the fair visage, and the hair
appealed to me so much that I have her in front of my eyes
and I shall always have her, whether I'm on a hill or on a bank.

I'll take my thoughts back to shore when
there isn't any green leaf on bay trees;
when my heart is at rest and my eyes are dry,
we'll see fire freezing and burning snow.
I haven't got as many hairs on my head
as the years I'd wait for that day.

But, since time flies and years flee,
so much that one reaches death in no time,
with brown or with white hair,
I'll follow the shadow of that sweet bay tree,
through the most searing sun and through snow,
until on my last day I close these eyes.

Such eyes as those have never been seen
either in our age or in remote ones,
such as the ones that consume me as snow in the sun;
whence a lachrymal shore proceeds,
which Love leads under the hard bay tree
which has diamond boughs and golden hair.

I fear my face and hair will change
before she looks at me with true mercy,
my idol carved in true bay wood;
since, if I am not wrong in counting, for seven years
I've gone sighing from shore to shore
day and night, through heat and through snow.

Fire within and candid snow outside,
alone with these thoughts, with a different hair,
weeping always I'll walk along every shore,
perhaps to stir some pity in the eyes
of somebody born a thousand years from now,
if a well-kept bay tree can live that long.

Gold and topaz, in the sun, on the snow
are no match for the blonde hair close to the eyes
that push my years, so early, to the last shore.

SESTINA OF THE TRAMP-ROYAL

SPEAKIN' in general, I 'ave tried 'em all
The 'appy roads that take you o'er the world.
Speakin' in general, I 'ave found them good
For such as cannot use one bed too long,
But must get 'ence, the same as I 'ave done,
An' go observin' matters till they die.

What do it matter where or 'ow we die,
So long as we've our 'ealth to watch it all –
The different ways that different things are done,
An' men an' women lovin' in this world;
Takin' our chances as they come along,
An' when they ain't, pretendin' they are good?

In cash or credit – no, it aren't no good;
You've to 'ave the 'abit or you'd die,
Unless you lived your life but one day long,
Nor didn't prophesy nor fret at all,
But drew your tucker some'ow from the world,
An' never bothered what you might ha' done.

But, Gawd, what things are they I 'aven't done?
I've turned my 'and to most, an' turned it good,
In various situations round the world
For 'im that doth not work must surely die;
But that's no reason man should labour all
'Is life on one same shift – life's none so long.

Therefore, from job to job I've moved along.
Pay couldn't 'old me when my time was done,
For something in my 'ead upset it all,
Till I 'ad dropped whatever 'twas for good,
An', out at sea, be'eld the dock-lights die,
An' met my mate – the wind that tramps the world!

It's like a book, I think, this bloomin' world,
Which you can read and care for just so long,
But presently you feel that you will die
Unless you get the page you're readin' done,
An' turn another – likely not so good;
But what you're after is to turn 'em all.

Gawd bless this world! Whatever she 'ath done –
Excep' When awful long – I've found it good.
So write, before I die, "'E liked it all!"
                    —Rudyard Kipling

LO ferm voler qu'el cor m'intra
 no'm pot ges becs escoissendre ni ongla
de lauzengier qui pert per mal dir s'arma;
e pus no l'aus batr'ab ram ni verja,
sivals a frau, lai on non aurai oncle,
jauzirai joi, en vergier o dins cambra.

Quan mi sove de la cambra
on a mon dan sai que nulhs om non intra
-ans me son tug plus que fraire ni oncle-
non ai membre no'm fremisca, neis l'ongla,
aissi cum fai l'enfas devant la verja:
tal paor ai no'l sia prop de l'arma.

Del cor li fos, non de l'arma,
e cossentis m'a celat dins sa cambra,
que plus mi nafra'l cor que colp de verja
qu'ar lo sieus sers lai ont ilh es non intra:
de lieis serai aisi cum carn e ongla
e non creirai castic d'amic ni d'oncle.

Anc la seror de mon oncle
non amei plus ni tan, per aquest'arma,
qu'aitan vezis cum es lo detz de l'ongla,
s'a lieis plagues, volgr'esser de sa cambra:
de me pot far l'amors qu'ins el cor m'intra
miels a son vol c'om fortz de frevol verja.

Pus floric la seca verja
ni de n'Adam foron nebot e oncle
tan fin'amors cum selha qu'el cor m'intra
non cug fos anc en cors no neis en arma:
on qu'eu estei, fors en plan o dins cambra,
mos cors no's part de lieis tan cum ten l'ongla.

Aissi s'empren e s'enongla
mos cors en lieis cum l'escors'en la verja,
qu'ilh m'es de joi tors e palais e cambra;
e non am tan paren, fraire ni oncle,
qu'en Paradis n'aura doble joi m'arma,
si ja nulhs hom per ben amar lai intra.

Arnaut tramet son chantar d'ongl'e d'oncle
a Grant Desiei, qui de sa verj'a l'arma,
son cledisat qu'apres dins cambra intra.
                    —Arnaut Daniel

The firm will that enters my heart
can't be scraped by beak nor by nail
of gossipmongers who damn, for ill speaking, their soul;
since I don't dare beat them with bough nor with rod,
at least, in secret, where there isn't any uncle,
I'll enjoy some pleasure, in the garden or in the room.

When I remember the room
where, to my scorn, I know no man enters
—rather, they are all to me more than brother or uncle—
I have no limb that doesn't shake, not even a fingernail,
just as a child when faced with the rod:
such is my fear of not being close to her soul.

Were I close to her body, not to her soul,
were she to let me hide in her room!
For it hurts my heart more than the stroke of a rod
that her [faithful] servant isn't there where she enters:
I'll be to her what a fingernail is to the flesh
and I won't follow the advice of friend nor of uncle.

Not even the sister of my uncle
I loved more, or as much, by this soul!
For, as the finger is close to the nail,
if she pleases, I want to be to her soul:
the love that enters my heart can do to me
more with its will than a strong man with a thin rod.

Since when the withered rod flourished
and from Adam sprung nephew and uncle,
a love as good as the one that enters my heart
I don't think has ever been in any body or soul:
wherever I am, out in the plains or inside, in the room,
my heart doesn't part from her more than a nail.

So sticks and is fixed like with a nail
my heart to her like the bark to the rod,
she's to me tower, palace and room;
and I don't love as much parent, brother or uncle,
and in Paradise my soul will have a double joy,
if anyone enters there out of good loving.

Arnaut sends this song about uncles and nails
to Great Desire, who holds the soul of his rod,
[it is] a framework-song that, once learned, enters the room.

The oldest French sextain known is the following one:

Le plus ardant de tous les Elemens
N'est si bouillant, alors que le Soleil,
Au fort d'esté le fier Lyon enflame,
Comme ie sens aux doux trets de ton œil,
Estre enflammée & bouillante mon ame:
Le triste corps languissant en tourmens.

A ces piteux travaux, à ces tourmens,
N'ont les hauts Cieux, & moins les Elemens,
Fait incliner, ou descendre mon ame:
Mais, comme on voit les rayons du Soleil
Eschauffer tout çà bas, ainsi ton œil
Rouant sur moi de plus en plus m'enflame.

Ie voy souvent Amour, lequel enflame,
Pour me donner plus gracieux tourmens,
Ser trets cuisans en ton flamboyant œil:
Lors memuant en deux purs elemens,
Le corps se fond en pleurs, quand ce Soleil
Empraint le feu plus ardemment en l'ame.

Vienne secher toute langoureuse ame,
(Si comme moy Amour trop fort l'enflame)
Ses tristes pleurs, aux rais de mon Soleil.
Vienne celuy, qui, comblé de tourmens,
Se pleint de Dieu, du Ciel, des Elemens,
Chercher confort au doux tret de cest œil,

Le doux regard, ou fier tret de cest œil
Fait ou ioyeuse, ou dolente toute ame,
Et temperez, ou non, les Elemens:
Außi c'est luy, qui rend froide, ou enflame,
L'occasion de tous ces miens tourmens,
Et qui m'est nuict obscure, ou cler Soleil.

Fuyant le iour de ce mien beau Soleil,
Tout m'est obscur, & rien ne voit mon œil,
Que dueil, ennui, & funebres tourmens:
Tourmens si grands, que ma douloureuse ame
Meut à pitié le Dieu, qui tant m'enflame,
Mesme le Ciel, & tous les Elemens.

Plustost ne soit resoult en Elemens
Ce corps, ny l'ame au Ciel sur le Soleil
Puisse saillir, que doux ne me soit l'œil,
Lequel m'enflame, & me tient en tourmens.
—Pontus de Tyard

The most fiery of all the elements
doesn't burn so much - when the Sun,
in Midsummer, is enflamed by the proud Leo -
as I feel, under the sweet darts of your eye,
myself being ignited and searing in my soul:
the body languishes tormented.

To these piteous trials, to these torments,
Neither the High Heavens nor the Elements
Have pushed or lowered my soul:
But, as one sees the rays of the Sun
Heat everything down here, so your eye,
Searing me, ignites me more and more.

I often see Love, who ignites,
That, in order to more graciously torment me,
Hides his arrows in your flaming eye:
Turning them into two pure elements,
The body melts in tears, when this Sun
Brands, searing even more the soul.

It comes to dry, my languid soul,
(since love too strongly ignites it)
its sad tears to the rays of my Sun.
It comes, full of torments,
To fill itself with God, with Heaven, with the Elements,
To look for comfort in the sweet darts of this eye.

The sweet look, or cruel dart of this eye
Turns to joy or to pain each soul,
And tempers, or not, the Elements:
The same way it is her, who freezes or ignites,
The cause of all my torments,
Who is to me dark night or fair Sun.

Away from the day of this beautiful Sun of mine
Everything is dark, and my eye sees nothing
But pain and spleen and funereal torments:
Torments so great that my dolorous soul
Moves to pity the God that so greatly ignites it,
Along with Heaven and with all the Elements.

Let rather be dissolved into the Elements
This body, and forbid that towards Heaven, under the Sun, my soul
Can ascend, rather than sweetness leaves the eye
That ignites me and gives me such torments.

This form is used in a plethora of other languages, including Catalan, Hungarian and Portuguese; in Spanish it seems to be undergoing a glorious time in South America, where both the Peruvian poet Carlos Germán Belli and the Venezuelan poetess Ana Nuño have recently written entire collections in this form.

Rondel

The rondel, often confused with the triolet (see below), is a French form of the fifteenth century, later taken up by the Parnasse poets, and mainly by the usual Banville, who wrote a whole collection in this style and several scattered pieces as well. Rondels exist in no other language, which is a shame; a true mediaeval example, written by Charles d'Orleans himself is this:

Le temps a laissé son manteau
De vent, de froidure et de pluie,
Et s'est vêtu de broderie,
De soleil luisant clair et beau.

Il n'y a bête ni oiseau
Qu'en son jargon ne chante ou crie.
Le temps a laissé son manteau
De vent, de froidure et de pluie.

Rivière, fontaine et ruisseau
Portent en livrée jolie
Gouttes d'argent d'orfèvrerie.
Chacun s'habille de nouveau,
Le temps a laissé son manteau

The weather has dropped its cloak
Of wind, of cold and of rain,
And has dressed itself in embroidery,
In sun, shining fair and beautiful.

There isn't any beast or bird
That doesn't sing or shout in its jargon.
The weather has dropped its cloak
Of wind, of cold and of rain.

River, fountain and stream
Carry, in jolly livery,
Drops of jewellery silver.
Everybody put new clothes on:
The weather has dropped its cloak.

As is quite apparent, although slight variations can be found, the rondel is a fairly homogeneous form, using thirteen lines in three stanzas based on only two rhymes. These are grouped according to the scheme (keeping the same conventions we have stated for the villanelle):

ABBA AB12 ABBA1

Rondels have been applied to practically everything, but most of the time they are used for descriptive pieces.

Rondeau

One of the most important French metres, the rondeau originated in the Middle Ages from some popular kind of sung piece, as did the homonymous instrumental classical musical form. Almost every French poet of the fifteenth – sixteenth century has written rondeaux galore, and in more modern times the usual Banville has written a cartload of them as well.

The rondeau has 15 lines, but only 13 verses, and these are built on two rhymes only. The two extra lines are explained as follows: the opening verse is divided into two hemistichs of arbitrary length, the first of which is inserted again after the 8th and 13th verse (or, if the Reader prefers, after the 8th and 14th line). No conditions are set about the nature of this hemistich: it need not rhyme, and it can be one word long, or take almost all of the first verse. Indicating the hemistich with h (lowercased because it is not a proper verse), the (fixed) rhyme scheme of a rondeau is:

AABBA AABh AABBAh

in case these notes don't appear to be clear, and they are likely not to, the Reader might wish to compare them to this Renaissance example Clément Marot:

> DEDANS Paris, ville jolie,
> Un jour, passant mélancolie,
> Je pris alliance nouvelle
> À la plus gaie demoiselle
> Qui soit d'ici en Italie.
>
> D'honnêteté elle est saisie,
> Et crois (selon ma fantaisie)
> Qu'il n'en est guère de plus belle
> Dedans Paris.
>
> Je ne la vous nommerai mie,
> Sinon que c'est ma grand'amie;
> Car l'alliance se fit telle
> Par un doux baiser que j'eus d'elle,
> Sans penser aucune infamie,
> Dedans Paris.
> ————Clément Marot

> *Inside Paris, jolly city,*
> *One day, abandoning melancholy,*
> *I formed a new bond*
> *With the merriest damsel*
> *one can find from here all the way to Italy.*
>
> *She is full of honesty*
> *And believe (according to my fancy)*
> *That there isn't anyone more beautiful*
> *Inside Paris.*
>
> *I shan't mention anything,*
> *Aside from [the fact that] she is my great friend;*
> *For our compact was formed*
> *Through a sweet kiss I had from her,*
> *Without thinking anything base,*
> *Inside Paris.*

Proper rondeaux are most common in French, but the form been used in this language for virtually *any* kind of poetry, from songs celebrating the seasons to elegies and dirges, to humorous pieces.

Rondeaux are all but alien to English poetry, however: in particular, several were written during the Victorian wake of proper formal poetry; W. E. Henley's 'What is to come' is one of them:

> WHAT is to come we know not. But we know
> That what has been was good – was good to show,
> Better to hide, and best of all to bear.
> We are the masters of the days that were;
> We have lived, we have loved, we have suffered…even so.
>
> Shall we not take the ebb who had the flow?
> Life was our friend? Now, if it be our foe –
> Dear, though it spoil and break us! – need we care
> What is to come?
>
> Let the great winds their worst and wildest blow,
> Or the gold weather round us mellow slow;
> We have fulfilled ourselves, and we can dare
> And we can conquer, though we may not share
> In the rich quiet of the afterglow
> What is to come.

Rondeaux, however rare, already existed in English also before queen Victoria's reign (Thomas Wyatt wrote several) and they certainly didn't fade into nothingness after her death: perhaps the most celebrated poem ever written by a Canadian, McCrae's 'In Flanders Fields' is clear evidence of this.

Roundel

The roundel was invented by C. A. Swinburne to summarise rondel, rondeau and perhaps triolet in one form suited to English; he wrote a whole book to better illustrate the concept, and had quite a following, including Ernest Dowson, whose 'Beyond' is an example, in his own country and age.

A roundel is built according to an

ABAh BABABAh

scheme (with the same conventions as above), therefore systematically avoiding couplets in order to achieve a more 'lyrical' effect; Swinburne's most famous one, and the only one you are likely to ever find in print is his programmatic one, 'The Roundel' (also note the awkward combination of completely anapaestic and amphibrachic lines):

> A roundel is wrought as a ring or a starbright sphere,
> With craft of delight and with cunning of sound unsought,
> That the heart of the hearer may smile if to pleasure his ear
> A roundel is wrought.
>
> Its jewel of music is carven of all or of aught -
> Love, laughter, or mourning -remembrance of rapture or fear-
> That fancy may fashion to hang in the ear of thought.
> As a bird's quick song runs round, and the hearts in us hear
> Pause answer to pause, and again the same strain caught,
> So moves the device whence, round as a pearl or tear,
>
> A roundel is wrought.

Rondeau Redoublé

For once, it is worth breaking the implicit rule of illustrating only English-related poetry to introduce this seriously minor, somewhat twisted and ex-clusively French metre, of which no more than a handful of examples (two of which, 'A Sylvie' and 'A Iris,' of course, by Banville) exist. The aim of this is showing how twisted and demanding poetic forms can be, even in Europe, the cradle of prosodic simplicity.

Technically speaking, a rondeau redoublé is made of six quatrains concluded by a hemistich (of exactly the same type as the one found in the rondeau form, and built on the first verse as well). The 24 verses, four of which are repeated twice (in the first stanza and as endings of stanzas 2–5) all belong to only two rhyme groups, *one of which must be feminine and the other mas-culine*. According to the usual conventions of this chapter, the rather tricky scheme of this form is:

ABAB BAB1 ABA2 BAB3 ABA4 BABAh

The most famous ancient rondeau redoublé is this didactic one by Vincent Voiture; since it is a 'poeticised' version of the rules given in the paragraph above we decline to translate it:

> Si l'on en trouve, on n'en trouvera guère
> De ces rondeaux qu'on nomme redoublés,
> Beaux et tournés d'une fine manière
> Si qu'à bon droit la plupart sont sifflés.
>
> A six quatrains les vers en sont réglés
> Sur double rime et d'espèce contraire.
> Rimes où soient douze mots accouplés,
> Si l'on en trouve, on n'en trouvera guère.
>
> Doit au surplus fermer son quaternaire
> Chacun de vous au premier assemblés,
> Pour varier toujours l'intercalaire
> De ces rondeaux qu'on nomme redoublés.
>
> Puis par un tour, tour des plus endiablés,
> Vont à pieds joints, sautant la pièce entière
> Les premiers mots qu'au bout vous enfilez,
> Beaux et tournés d'une fine manière.
>
> Dame Paresse, à parler sans mystère,
> Tient nos rimeurs de sa cape affublés:
> Tout ce qui gêne est sûr de leur déplaire,
> Si qu'à bon droit la plupart sont sifflés.
>
> Ceux qui de gloire étaient jadis comblés,
> Par beau labeur en gagnaient le salaire:
> Ces forts esprits, aujourd'hui cherchez-les;
> Signe de croix on aura lieu de faire
> Si l'on en trouve.

This form is too rare for the Present Author to state anything general on its usage; even Voiture laments that 'the largest majority [of these poems] is flawed'. Some light might come from the fact that it is actually one of the French versions of a more widespread form, the glose, described in detail in Chapter V.

Triolet

Again a mainly French metre, again one based on two rhyming groups and a
verse repeated thrice, the triolet, a form of eight lines disposed according to a

   ABA1 AB12

scheme, is the ancient French equivalent of a limerick (see the Conclusions),
used mainly for satirical purposes, as shown in this quite typical example by
Villon:

> Jenin l'Avenu,
> Va-t-en aux estuves;
> Et toy la venu,
> Jenin l'Avenu,
>
> Si te lave nu
> Et tu baigne es cuves.
> Jenin l'Avenu,
> Va-t-en aux estuves.

> *Little John the Pretentious,*
> *Go to the Baths;*
> *And when you are there,*
> *Little John the Pretentious,*
>
> *Then wash yourself naked,*
> *Take a bath in the tubs.*
> *Little John the Pretentious,*
> *Go to the Baths.*

Exceptions to this character exist, however, as the somewhat intimate 'Mon
coeur s'ébat en odorant la rose' by Jean Froissart shows. Banville and other
Parnasse poets wrote a cornucopia of poems in this form; the Reader that
has suddenly fallen in love with it can find all he needs in the former's *Odes
funambulesques*.

English triolets were written, not surprisingly, by Henley and Austin Dob-
son: here is *A Kiss*, by the latter:

> Rose kissed me to-day.
> Will she kiss me tomorrow?
> Let it be as it may,
> Rose kissed me today.

But the pleasure gives way
To a savour of sorrow;
Rose kissed me to-day,
Will she kiss me tomorrow?

As a final note, *triolets, rondels and similar pieces are often rudely grouped under the name of rondeaux.* This is due mainly to the fact that there are several pieces that resemble them without exactly fitting in any of the schemes above, as the magnificent 'Vous qui vivez à présent en ce monde' by E. Deschamps.

To add further confusion to the matter, some English-speaking authors tend to call 'rondeau' any friskily-flowing poem, such as this one (in trochees, no less):

Jenny kissed me when we met,
Jumping from the chair she sat in;
Time, you thief, who love to get
Sweets into your list, put that in:
Say I'm weary, say I'm sad,
Say that health and wealth have missed me,
Say I'm growing old, but add,
Jenny kissed me.

—Leigh Hunt

But the times of deception is over: the Reader, now shielded by the Present Guide, will never be fooled anymore by these wiles.

Sources and further reading

Again, the Reader should turn back to Chapter I for a list of references; a number of books treat single forms in various languages, and, above all, the sonnet. Should the reader feel like being bored to tears, he would find Fuller, H. *The Sonnet* (London: Methuen & Co., 1973), Legman, G. *The Limerick* (New York: Wings Books, 1969) and McFarland, R. E. *The Villanelle: The Evolution of a Poetic Form* (Moscow: Idaho Research Foundation, 1988) perfect for the task. Reportedly (the Present Author never having been so lucky), the rare Cohen, H. *Lyric Forms from France: Their History and Their Use.* (New York: Harcourt, Brace and Company, 1922), dealing with the Ballade, Chant Royal, Rondeau, Triolet, Villanelle, and Sestina in England and France, is a more fascinating reading. Those concerned with the evolution of themes, and in particular with those of decadent pieces, could consult Binni, W. *La poetica del decadentismo* (Firenze: Sansoni, 1968).

IV. Open Forms

Stanza Theory and Conventions

There are three ways to handle rhymes and stanzas in European poetry, although only the easiest one has any importance in classic English poetry. Three of these techniques are usually referred to by their Provençal name, for reasons that are unclear to anybody but some long-dead Occitanic scholar.

The first one is called coblas continuadas and in it any set of rhymed endings is restricted to a single stanza and found nowhere else; that means that any rhyming pattern is resumed in the next stanza with a different set and generally no reference to the preceding one. In fewer words, each line of the stanza rhymes with other lines within the same stanza and with nothing else. This is the common way of writing poems in English and, in most cases, also in all modern European languages.

As virtually any rhymed English poem you can quickly think of falls in this category, the Present Author refrains from bothering you with one more example and for that you should be grateful to Him for centuries to come.

A second technique is called *coblas capcaudadas* and in it one or more rhymes are carried from one stanza to the following one (they go through two stanzas only and not the whole work). This use is not particularly common in European literature and the Present Author describes it mainly out of sheer sadism.

A third and even rarer one, *coblas unissonantis* consists in keeping the same rhymes in exactly the same positions in all stanzas.

Last but not least there is the *rime en kyrielle*, which consists in periodically repeating the same line. It is to be noted that some of the forms we shall analyse sometimes do not fall precisely in any one of these groups, but they can usually be assimilated to them. Furthermore, two or more techniques can be combined in the same poem: a piece written entirely in rime en kyrielle would just be a silly repetition of the same thing, for example, so that the reoccurring verses are complemented by new ones which are connected to them according to one, or more, of the three other ways of arranging them.

All this may seem complicated, but the practical cases will immediately show how elementary the underlying concepts are. What actually matters is the understanding that these four simple techniques, applied according to the taste of the poet, produce the endless variety of classic verse, and that sometimes theoretical attempts at classifying dozens of different verse forms appear to be idle and vain when one compares these to a more general idea. The case of the ode, here, is by far the most prominent.

Coblas Continuadas

Ode

Under this tattered flag are grouped an endless number of poems made of equal stanzas in coblas continuadas. Such a poem need not be always called an 'ode', and oftentimes it is not even referred to as a verse form in itself; the rules generally applied in its construction are:

- Stanzas are rhymed as coblas continuadas (see above)

- Each line must be rhymed with at least another line in the same stanza

- Each stanza is a sequence of the same types of verses as the others, in the same order and with the same rhyme scheme

In most compositions of this type, at least in English, the same kind of verse (in the sense of line structure) is used throughout all the stanza (and therefore, as an application of rule 3, throughout all the poem); if it is iambic pentameter, the name often used for this metre becomes *elegiac stanza*.

Odes (according to our definition) have existed in all modern languages of Western Europe and in several others, including mediaeval Latin, for at least seven centuries, and have been used to treat almost any topic, employing almost any style.

Some examples follow; in Provençal poetry this form is almost always followed by an envoi (rhymed as the last part of the last stanza), as in the Arnaut Daniel's example below.

QUAN CHAI la fuelha
dels aussors entressims
el freg s'erguelha
don seca 'l vais e'l vims,
del dous refrims
vei sordezir la bruelha:
mais ieu sui prims
d'Amor qui que s'en tuelha.

Tot quan es gela,
mas ieu no puesc frezir
qu'amors novela
mi fa'l cor reverdir;
non dei fremir
qu'Amors mi cuebr'em cela
em fai tenir
ma valor em capdela

Bona es vida
pus Joia la mante
quei tals n'escrida
qui ges non vai tam be;
no sai de re
coreillar m'escarida
que per ma fe
de mielhs ai ma partida.

De drudaria
no'm sai de re blasmar,
qu'autrui paria
trastorn en reirazar;
geb as sa par
no sai doblar m'amia
q'una non par
que segonda no'l sia

No vuelh s'asemble
mos cors ab autr'amor
si qu'eu ja'l m'emble
ni volva'l cap alhor:
no ai paor
que ja selh de Pontremble
n'aia gensor
de lieis ni que la semble.

Tant es per genta
selha que'm te joios
las gensors trenta
vens de belhas faisos:
ben es razos
doncas que mos chans senta
quar es tan pros
e de ric pretz manenta.

Vai t'en chanzos,
denan lei ti presenta,
que s'ill no fos
no'i meir'Arnautz s'ententa.
                    —Arnaut Daniel

When the leaf sings
from the highest peaks
and the cold rises
withering hazelnut and willow,
of its sweet refrains
I see the wood grow dumb:
but I'm close to love,
whoever might abandon it.

Everything is frozen,
but I cannot freeze
because a love affair
makes my heart lush again;
I should not shiver
since Love covers and hides me
and makes me preserve
my worth, and leads me.

Life is good,
if joy holds it
(though some complain,
whose things do not go well);
I don't know how
to accuse my lot
since, by my troth,
I have my share of the best.

As of flirting,
I don't know what to blame,
and of others
I spurn the company;
since of all her peers
no one is like mine
since no one seems to exist
who does not rank lower than her.

I don't want my heart
to seek another love
lest she'd flee me
and turn her head elsewhere:
I have no fear
that not even the one from Pontremoli
has one worthier
than her, or so it seems.

She's so kind,
the one that keeps me in joy,
that the kindest thirty
she beats, with her fair look:
that's a good reason
for her to hear my songs
because she's so noble
and so preciously deserving.

Go, then, song,
show before her:
if it were not so
you wouldn't deserve Arnaut's toil.

TO MAYSTRES ISABELL KNYGHT

But if I sholde aquyte your kyndnes,
Els saye ye myght
That in me were grete blyndnes,
I for to be so myndles,
And cowde not wryght
Of Isabell Knyght.

It is not my custome nor my gyse
To leve behynde
Her that is bothe womanly and wyse,
And specyally which glad was to devyse
The menes to fynde
To please my mynde,

In helpyng to warke my laurell grene
With sylke and golde.
Galathea, the made well besene,
Was never halfe so fayre, as I wene,
Whiche was extolde
A thowsande folde

By Maro, the Mantuan prudent,
Who list to rede
But, and I had leyser competent,
I coude shew you suche a presedent
In very dede
How ye excede.

—John Skelton

COMPLAINTE SUR CERTAINS ENNUIS

Un couchant des Cosmogonies!
Ah! que la Vie est quotidienne...
Et, du plus vrai qu'on se souvienne,
Comme on fut piètre et sans génie...

On voudrait s'avouer des choses,
Dont on s'étonnerait en route,
Qui feraient une fois pour toutes !
Qu'on s'entendrait à travers poses.

On voudrait saigner le Silence,
Secouer l'exil des causeries;
Et non ! ces dames sont aigries
Par des questions de préséance.

Elles boudent là, l'air capable.
Et, sous le ciel, plus d'un s'explique,
Par quel gâchis suresthétique
Ces êtres-là sont adorables.

Justement, une nous appelle,
Pour l'aider à chercher sa bague,
Perdue (où dans ce terrain vague?)
Un souvenir d'AMOUR, dit-elle!

Ces êtres-là sont adorables!
                            —Jules Laforgue

COMPLAINT OVER SOME NUISANCES
A sunset of Cosmogonies!
Ah, how commonplace life is!
and the truest thing we remember
is how we were unglorious and devoid of genius...

We would like to confess things
such as would astonish on the way
and such as would make it so—once and for all!—
that we can understand each other through our poses.

We would like to bleed the Silence,
shake the exile of the chit-chat;
but no! these ladies have turned sour
over matters of precedence.

They pout there, with a presumptuous attitude.
And, under Heaven, several understand
which over-esthetical garble makes it so that
these beings are so adorable.

Right now one calls for us
to help her look for her ring,
lost (where, in this uncertain ground?)
a keepsake of LOVE, she says!

These beings are so adorable!

For an Italian example, refer to the Guittone piece given in Chapter II; a Spanish one, by Machado can be found in Chapter VIII. The name 'ode' is also often hung onto poems that do not comply to the rules given here, while most of the poems that do are not called odes. We would like to instil even in the thickest skull the fact we have *somewhat arbitrarily*, albeit based on quite a number of examples, chosen this name for this form. Odes are so common that they have been, and still are, used for any kind of poetry; in this definition of ode can be included the *Spenserian stanza* mentioned in the versification chapter, Chaucer's *rhyme royal*, the Italian *ottava rima* and many, many other minor forms. It is important that it is understood that these are only particular applications of a more general concept that can, and does, produce an infinite variety. More recently (but with some important exceptions) the custom has become to employ homogeneous verses throughout all the stanzas, maiming the metre not a little, and more recently still, to use four-line stanzas only, as in Arthur Rimbaud's 'Le Bateau ivre', thus definitely killing it. From the ashes of this latter cremation, in a sense, the ballad has risen (needless to say, the Present Writer is aware this is not *historically* exact, but it does make sense phylogenetically).

Rhyming Couplet

The easiest, basest kind of coblas continuadas (and of verse in general) is the rhyming couplet. Dearly loved by rhymesters and pop singers of every age, this metre has become so common so quickly it actually features an impressive amount of decent, good and even masterly pieces. It is impossible to track back this verse to its origins, which are probably to be found in the transition of Latin from a quantitative to an inflected language, and maybe even before that (hints of rhyming can be seen in some perfectly classic hexameters), but certainly it was already obsolete when the first Romance poems we know were written; in spite of that, rhyming couplets enjoyed an unrivalled popularity in the late Middle Ages, when they became the metre of the French and English lay. A rhyming couplet is simply a couple of verses of the same type with the same rhyme; several of these units are filed, without necessarily having any logical or phonetic interruption between each other. Perhaps the true masterpiece of the kind is Verlaine's 'Effet de nuit':

La nuit. La pluie. Un ciel blafard que déchiquette
De flèches et de tours à jour la silhouette
D'une ville gothique éteinte au lointain gris.
La plaine. Un gibet plein de pendus rabougris
Secoués par le bec avide des corneilles
Et dansant dans l'air noir des gigues nonpareilles,
Tandis que leurs pieds sont la pâture des loups.
Quelques buissons d'épine épars, et quelques houx
Dressant l'horreur de leur feuillage à droite, à gauche,
Sur le fuligineux fouillis d'un fond d'ébauche.
Et puis, autour de trois livides prisonniers
Qui vont pieds nus, un gros de hauts pertuisaniers
En marche, et leurs fers droits, comme des fers de herse,
Luisent à contresens des lances de l'averse.

Night. Rain. A sallow sky that tatters
from spires and towers the outline
of a Gothic town lost in the faraway grey.
The plain. A gibbet hung full with shrivelled corpses
Shaken by the greedy beaks of the ravens
And dancing unmatched gigues through the black air,
While their feet are the meal of wolves.
Some sparse thornbrush and some holly
Making the horror of their foliage stand to the right, to the left,
Against the sooty confusion of a sketch.
And then, around three livid prisoners
That go barefoot, a great host of partisan-bearers
Marching, with their weapons upright, like harrow-teeth
Gleaming opposite to the spears of the rain.

English examples are found throughout all the history of British literature, from Chaucer to Eliot, and particularly among the shallowest Cavalier poets; Marlowe's translations of Ovid's Elegies are an example of a less deleterious use of the form.

Couplets are used in classic European poetry basically only in English and French; they are avoided in Italian because they sound somewhat sing-songy, and Provençal authors seemed to think of them as too primitive a device. No Spanish example is known to the Present Author, who, from the abysms of His ignorance of the language, cannot say whether any exist.

Starting from the middle of the nineteenth century, an increasing number of authors wrote rhyming couplets composed of verses of arbitrary length; this form, of which the best examples are perhaps to be found in Ogden Nash's work, is not strictly a type of coblas continuadas anymore.

Song

This is merely the name given by most English authors to odes (in the sense defined above) made mostly of, or to couplets made exclusively of, verses with an odd number of metrical syllables (which, as already stated in Chapter I, sound sing-songy). Most rock and country lyrics fit in this definition as well.

This is probably the first prosody manual ever, and maybe the last, to reveal this truth to the people.

Songs are fairly common, often treat of springtime and/or love, and tend to be pointless and annoying. Songs, or fragments of them, are often included in Renaissance plays in a vain effort to wake up the onlooker: even the gloomiest Webster at times resorts to this childish device as in *The Duchess of Malfi* (albeit he manages to be anamorphic even in that: he lengthens some verses and shortens others while keeping the general effect):

> Hark now every thing is still
> The screech-owl and whistler still
> Call upon our Dame, aloud
> And bid her quick don her shroud.
> Much you had of land and rent,
> Your length in clay's now competent.
> A long war disturb'd your mind,
> Here your perfect peace is sign'd.
> Of what is't fools make such vain keeping?
> Sin their conception, their birth weeping

To conclude, here is a very famous and very typical Italian poetic song (namely, a 'scherzo', literally 'prank' – but the two terms are equivalent) by Chiabrera, a Mannerist poet whose pieces have several times been used as lyrics in the late Renaissance:

BELLE rose porporine
che tra spine
sull'aurora non aprite;
ma, ministre degli amori,
bei tesori
di bei denti custodite:

Dite, rose prezïose,
amorose;
dite, ond'è, che s'io m'affiso
nel bel guardo vivo ardente,
voi repente
disciogliete un bel sorriso?

E' ciò forse per aïta
di mia vita,
che non regge alle vostr'ire?
O pur è perché voi siete
tutte liete,
me mirando in sul morire?

Belle rose, o feritate,
o pietate
del sì far la cagion sia,
io vo' dire in nuovi modi
vostre lodi,
ma ridete tuttavia.

Se bel rio, se bell'auretta
dell'erbetta
sul mattin mormorando erra;
se di fiori un praticello
si fa bello;
noi diciam: ride la terra.

Quando avvien che un zefiretto
per diletto
bagni il piè nell'onde chiare,
sicché l'acqua in sulla rena
scherzi appena;
noi diciam che ride il mare.

Se giammai tra fior vermigli
se tra gigli
vesta l'alba un aureo velo;
e su rote di zaffiro
move in giro;
noi diciam che ride il cielo.

Ben è ver, quand'è giocondo
ride il mondo,
ride il ciel quand'è gioioso:
ben è ver; ma non san poi
come voi
fare un riso grazïoso.

Beautiful, purple roses
that, among thorns,
don't open in the dawn;
but, ministers of love,
you hold beautiful treasures
among beautiful teeth:

Tell me, precious roses,
loving roses;
Tell me, how come that if I look
into the living fire of those eyes
all of a sudden you
produce a smile?

Is it perchance to help
my life,
which can't bear your anger?
Or is it because you are
all happy
to see me dying?

Beautiful roses, whether it is out of cruelty
or out of mercy
that you act so,
I want to find new ways
to praise you
and you laugh all the same.

If a beautiful rill or a beautiful gust
through the grass
wanders in the morning;
if with flowers a lawn
is adorned;
we say: the earth is smiling.

Should it happen that a zephyr
amusingly
sinks its feet in the clear waves
so that the water on the sand
barely plays;
we say: the sea is smiling.

If ever among crimson flowers
among lilies
dawn dons a golden veil
and on sapphire wheels
revolves around;
we say: the sky is smiling.

It is true, when it is gay
the world smiles,
the sky smiles when it is playful:
it is true, but neither can
smile
as graciously as you do.

Epigram

Epigrams are not too clearly defined as a form; they have ancient origins, being already common in decadent Latin authors, particularly Seneca and Martial. Through the influence of the latter author, epigrams were introduced in English as a type of short, rhymed metre used for trenchant humour, personal attacks, and/or triviality.

Prosodically speaking, epigrams generally are made of a single stanza, often a short one; since the original Latin ones are written in distichs, English ones tend to be either made of couplets of uniform verses, or of alternated patterns of one longer and one shorter verse.

An example of the former, uniform type is provided by Sir John Har-rington's translation of Martial's *To One That Had Meat Ill Dressed*:

> KING Mithridate to poysons so inur'd him
> As deadly poysons damage non procur'd him
> So you to stale vnsauorie foode and durtie,
> are so inur'd, as famine ne're can hurt yee.

Whereas the second, more interesting type is well illustrated by the Earl of Rochester's *On Charles II*:

> God bless our Good and Gracious King,
> Whose Promise none relies on;
> Who never said a Foolish Thing,
> Nor ever did a Wise One.

Famous epigrams are by John Donne and Ben Jonson; the latter was quite prone to use this otherwise polemical form for flattery, as can be well shown in this example:

> Donne, the delight of Phoebus and each Muse
> Who, to thy one, all other brains refuse;
> Whose every work of thy most early wit
> Came forth example, and remains so yet;
> Longer a-knowing than most wits do live;
> And which no affection praise enough can give!
> To it, thy language, letters, arts, best life,
> Which might with half mankind maintain a strife.
> All which I meant to praise, and yet I would;
> But leave, because I cannot as I should!

Ballad

As hinted above, the ballad is basically a barbaric involution of an ode with four lines in each stanza. The various degrees of the transition (Darwin, envy me!) are apparent in some of Robert Burn's works. Its verses usually have an easy but irregular rhythm, and they often either have eight metric syllables or four beats (or both features). The second line of each stanza rimes with the fourth, while the first and third are unrhymed (or rime with each other, but that is rare); the last one is sometimes shorter than the other three, carrying only three beats (or six metric syllables, or both).

Ballads are used for storytelling, usually for melancholic and corny tales about damsels and knights. Well-crafted samples of this typically eighteenth-century form sound somewhat archaic, so that the layman uses to think it originated in mediaeval ages (during which, instead, the world 'unrhymed' was never applied to poetry by any sane man).

Ballads are exclusive to English and the Scottish (non Celtic) dialect; Coleridge was certainly thinking of them when writing his *Rhyme of the Ancient Marineer*, while Keats' *La Belle Dame Sans Merci* is an explicit example:

> Ah, what can ail thee, wretched wight,
> Alone and palely loitering;
> The sedge is withered from the lake,
> And no birds sing.
>
> Ah, what can ail thee, wretched wight,
> So haggard and so woe-begone?
> The squirrel's granary is full,
> And the harvest's done.
>
> I see a lily on thy brow,
> With anguish moist and fever dew;
> And on thy cheek a fading rose
> Fast withereth too.
>
> I met a lady in the meads
> Full beautiful, a faery's child;
> Her hair was long, her foot was light,
> And her eyes were wild.
>
> I set her on my pacing steed,
> And nothing else saw all day long;
> For sideways would she lean, and sing
> A faery's song.
>
> I made a garland for her head,
> And bracelets too, and fragrant zone;
> She looked at me as she did love,
> And made sweet moan.
>
> She found me roots of relish sweet,
> And honey wild, and manna dew;
> And sure in language strange she said,
> I love thee true.

She took me to her elfin grot,
And there she gazed and sighed deep,
And there I shut her wild sad eyes-
So kissed to sleep.

And there we slumbered on the moss,
And there I dreamed, ah woe betide,
The latest dream I ever dreamed
On the cold hill side.

I saw pale kings, and princes too,
Pale warriors, death-pale were they all;
Who cried - "La belle Dame sans merci
Hath thee in thrall!"

I saw their starved lips in the gloam
With horrid warning gaped wide,
And I awoke, and found me here
On the cold hill side.

And this is why I sojourn here
Alone and palely loitering,
Though the sedge is withered from the lake,
And no birds sing.

Coblas Capifinidas

Terza Rima

Mathematically speaking, terza rima is the simplest possible application of the concept of coblas capifinidas: it is composed of a sequence of stanzas of three verses of the same type each, where the two outer ones rhyme with each other, while the inner one rhymes with the first (and then also with the last) line of the next stanza, thus creating a pattern of the type:

ABA BCB CDC DED ...

The chain is concluded by a single line rhyming with the middle one of the last full stanza, creating the scheme:

... WXW XYX YZY Z

This metre is so famous it is even mentioned in the literature courses of some American universities; we owe this to Dante, who invented it and used it to write the whole *Divina commedia*. It has been employed ever since in Italian for medium-to-very-long pieces, although its popularity has sharply declined after the baroque age. In English it began being appreciated during the Renaissance by Italy-loving authors, and lasted until the age of those believing things went bump in the night in places as boring as Otranto. In French, the form was used by Parnasse and decadent poets (who tried just everything, the more mediaeval the better).

Terze rime also exist in Spanish, but, as far as the Present Author knows, concern no other language than those mentioned, and can well be exemplified by:

> QUEST'È il piovan Arlotto e non gli tocca
> il nome indarno; né fu posto al vento
> sì come nelle secchie mai die' in brocca.
>
> Costui non s'inginocchia al Sacramento
> quando si lieva, se non v'è buon vino,
> perché non crede che Iddio vi sia drento.
>
> E come già per miracol divino
> Iosuè fermò il sol contra natura,
> così costui e insieme un suo vicino,
>
> fermò la notte tenebrosa e scura;
> e scambioron un dì, e se ben miro,
> e la notte seguente: odi sciagura!
>
> Il primo dì un certo armaro aprîro,
> pensando loro una finestra aprire;
> scuro vedendo, al letto rifuggîro.
>
> Volle Iddio che levossi da dormire
> quel della casa e mostrò loro il giorno,
> che così ben si potevon morire:
>
> e così il terzo giorno resuscitorno,
> benché pria che 'l secondo fussin desti,
> perché dormendo de' tre dì toccorno.
> —Lorenzo de' Medici

This is the Great Debauched and his nickname
is not in vain; and he was never put out to dry
since he has never touched water.

He does not kneel in church
when he gets up, unless there is good wine
'cause otherwise he doesn't believe God to be in it.

And with a divine miracle alike to
Joshua's, who stopped the sun against nature,
this man, together with a neighbour

stopped the dim, dark night;
they traded a day, unless I'm wrong,
with the following night: listen to this!

The first day they opened some cupboard,
thinking they were opening a window;
seeing it was dark, they went back to bed.

For God's grace, their landlord
woke up and showed them the day,
otherwise, they could well have died:

and so the third day they were resurrected,
albeit they had been awake two days before,
since they slept for three full days.

The boughs, the boughs are bare enough
But earth has never felt the snow.
Frost-furred our ivies are and rough

With bills of rime the brambles show.
The hoarse leaves crawl on hissing ground
Because the sighing wind is low.

But if the rain-blasts be unbound
And from dank feathers wring the drops
The clogged brook runs with choking sound

Kneading the mounded mire that stops
His channel under clammy coats
Of foliage fallen in the copse.

A simple passage of weak notes
Is all the winter bird dare try.
The bugle moon by daylight floats

So glassy white about the sky,
So like a berg of hyaline,
And pencilled blue so daintily,

I never saw her so divine.
But through black branches, rarely dressed
In scarves of silky hot and shine,

The webbed and the watery west
Where yonder crimson fireball sets
Looks laid for feasting and for rest.

I see long reefs of violets
In beryl-covered ferns so dim,
A gold-water Pactolus frets

It's brindled wharves and yellow brim,
The waxen colours weepand run,
And slendering to his burning rim

Into the flat blue mist the sun
Drops out and the day is done.
                    —Gerard Manley Hopkins

LA LYRE D'ORPHÉE

A sa voix se leva le prince des Aèdes
et son Luth animé, plein de souffles ardents,
si douloureusement vibra sous ses doigts raides,

que les tigres rayés et les lions grondants
le suivaient, attendris, et lui faisant cortège,
doux, avec des lambeaux de chair entre les dents.

Chœur monstrueux conduit par un divin Chorège!
Les grands pins, pour mieux voir l'étrange défilé,
en cadence inclinaient leurs fronts chargés de neige.

Les gouttes de son sang sur le Luth étoilé
brillaient. Charmant sa peine au son des notes lentes,
l'Aède, fils du ciel, se sentit consolé:

car tout son cœur chantait dans les cordes sanglantes.
— Jules Lemaître

ORPHEUS' LYRE
At his voice rose the prince of Bards
and his animated lute, full of burning sighs,
vibrates so painfully, under his stiff fingers,

that the striped tigers and the growling lions
followed him, merciful, like his train,
sweet, with pieces of flesh among their teeth.

Monstrous choir lead by a divine dancer!
The great pines, in order to see better the odd masque,
bent in turn their snow-laden brows.

The drops of his blood, over the starry lute,
shone. Charming his pain with the sound of the slow notes,
the Bard, son of Heaven, felt consoled:

since his whole heart sung in the bleeding strings.

CARTA PARA ARIAS MONTANO (excerpt):

Montano, cuyo nombre es la primera
estrellada señal por do camina
el sol el cerco oblicuo de la esfera,

nombrado así por voluntad divina,
para mostrar que en ti comienza Apolo
la luz de su celeste disciplina:

yo soy un hombre desvalido y solo,
expuesto al duro hado cual marchita
hoja al rigor del descortés Eolo;

mi vida temporal anda precita
dentro el infierno del común trafago
que siempre añade un mal y un bien nos quita.

Oficio militar profeso y hago,
baja condenación de mi ventura
que al alma dos infiernos da por pago.

Los huesos y la sangre que natura
me dio para vivir, no poca parte
dellos y della he dado a la locura,

mientras el pecho al desenvuelto Marte
tan libre di que sin mi daño puede,
hablando la verdad, ser muda el arte.

Y el rico galardón que se concede
a mi (llámola así) ciega porfía
es que por ciego y porfiado quede.

No digo más sobre esto, que podría
cosas decir que un mármol deshiciese
en el piadoso humor que el ojo envía,

y callaré las causas de interese,
no sé si justo o injusto, que en alguno
hubo porque mi mal más largo fuese.

. .   .   .   .   .

—Francisco de Aldana

*LETTER TO ARIAS MONTANO ABOUT THE CONTEMPLATION OF
GOD AND ITS REQUISITES*

*Montano, whose name is the first
starry sign through which the sun
treads the slanted circle of the sphere,*

*thus named by God's will,
to show that in you Apollo commences
the light of his celestial discipline:*

*I am a lone, defenceless man,
exposed to the harsh fates just as a withered
leaf [is] to the duress of unkind Aeolus;*

*my mundane life goes on, reprobate,
into the hell of everyday business
that always adds an evil and takes away a boon.*

*I engage in the military profession,
low condemnation of my fortune,
that always repays soul with two hells.*

The bones and the blood, that Nature
gave me to live with, not a little
of them and of it I have given away to folly,

while my chest [I have given] to breezy Mars
so freely that art can be dumb,
to tell the truth, without much harm to me.

And the rich meed awarded
to my (let's call it so) blind obduracy
is remaining obdurate and blind.

I shan't say anything else about this, since I could
say things that would melt a marble statue
into the piteous fluid the eye produces,

and I'll omit the causes of interest,
I don't know whether rightful or not, that somebody
had in making me labour longer.

Terze rime are another extremely flexible device: albeit they were originally created for narrative poetry, they have been successfully employed for any genre, from lyricism to satire.

Pantoum

Until now, in this chapter, we have mostly been frolicking around with forms one can easily use to write a list of his desiderata at the greengrocer's shop down the lane. The Present Author is actually able to do that in a pantoum as well (although He is keeping to His promise not to flaunt His skill and shan't do it here), but freely admits it takes some time and concentration.

The pantoum is a peculiarly abstruse classic Malay open form that was introduced into French poetry by Hugo, through a translation in his 'Orientales'; the metre is so difficult that, up to today there is no example in Western literature that fits *exactly* its definition, which is the following:

- Each verse line must have eight syllables

- A pantoum is made of stanzas of four lines each

- The first line must rhyme with the fourth, and the second must rime with the third

- The *second* line of each stanza must be used as the *first* line of the next stanza

- The *fourth* line of each stanza must be used as the *third* line of the next stanza

- The first line of the first stanza must be used as the last line of the last stanza

From these conditions follow some logical consequences, which are reported here for the mentally lazy reader:

- A pantoum, most like a rondeau, is based on two rhyming groups only

- A pantoum has an odd number of stanzas

- A pantoum is damn hard to write properly

Practically speaking, in European languages, nobody has ever cared about point 1, point 6 is not that popular either, and point 3 is consented to only by the most skilled writers. Assuming we are dealing with one of these, the scheme for this metre, with the usual conventions, becomes:

ABBA 2A4B 6B8A ...

A piece in this style, and probably the most popular pantoum ever written, is Baudelaire's 'Harmonie du soir':

> Voici venir les temps où vibrant sur sa tige
> Chaque fleur s'évapore ainsi qu'un encensoir;
> Les sons et les parfums tournent dans l'air du soir;
> Valse mélancolique et langoureux vertige!
>
> Chaque fleur s'évapore ainsi qu'un encensoir;
> Le violon frémit comme un coeur qu'on afflige;
> Valse mélancolique et langoureux vertige!
> Le ciel est triste et beau comme un grand reposoir.

Le violon frémit comme un coeur qu'on afflige,
Un coeur tendre, qui hait le néant vaste et noir!
Le ciel est triste et beau comme un grand reposoir
Le soleil s'est noyé dans son sang qui se fige.

Un coeur tendre, qui hait le néant vaste et noir!
Du passé lumineux recueille tout vestige!
Le soleil s'est noyé dans son sang qui se fige...
Ton souvenir en moi luit comme un ostensoir!

Now comes the time when, vibrating on its stem
Each flower evaporates like a censer;
The sounds and perfumes swirl in the evening air
Melancholy waltz and languid vertigo!

Each flower evaporates like a censer;
The violin shivers like a tormented heart;
Melancholy waltz and languid vertigo!
The sky is sad and beautiful like a great altar.

The violin shivers like a tormented heart,
A tender heart that hates the vast, black void!
The sky is sad and beautiful like a great altar
The sun has drowned itself in its own congealing blood.

A tender heart that hates the vast, black void!
Recollect all the spoils of the luminous past!
The sun has drowned itself in its own congealing blood...
Your memory shines in me like an altar!

A more relaxed, and therefore more popular, convention rhymes the first line with the third and the second with the fourth, producing a completely different effect, but at least dramatically easing the scheme, which becomes:

ABAB 2C4C 6D8D ...

Albeit obviously a simplification, this second definition of pantoum is used by such poets as Banville and Laforgue and, in the United Kingdom, by Henry Austin Dobson:

IN TOWN

"The blue fly sung in the pane" –TENNYSON

Toiling in Town now is "horrid,"
(There is that woman again !)—
June in the zenith is torrid,
Thought gets dry in the brain.

There is that woman again :
"Strawberries ! fourpence a pottle !"
Thought gets dry in the brain ;
Ink gets dry in the bottle.

"Strawberries ! fourpence a pottle !"
Oh for the green of a lane !—
Ink gets dry in the bottle ;
"Buzz" goes a fly in the pane !

Oh for the green of a lane,
Where one might lie and be lazy !
"Buzz" goes a fly in the pane ;
Bluebottles drive me crazy !

Where one might lie and be lazy,
Careless of Town and all in it !—
Bluebottles drive me crazy :
I shall go mad in a minute !

Careless of Town and all in it,
With some one to soothe and to still you ;—
I shall go mad in a minute ;
Bluebottle, then I shall kill you !

With some one to soothe and to still you,
As only one's feminine kin do,—
Bluebottle, then I shall kill you :
There now ! I've broken the window !

As only one's feminine kin do,—
Some muslin-clad Mabel or May !–
There now ! I've broken the window !
Bluebottle's off and away !

Some muslin-clad Mabel or May,
To dash one with eau de Cologne ;–
Bluebottle's off and away ;
And why should I stay here alone !

To dash one with eau de Cologne,
All over one's eminent forehead ;—
And why should I stay here alone !
Toiling in Town now is "horrid,"

A quite widespread opinion in some English-speaking countries holds pantoums are only a mean by which one can write a poem of 2n+4 lines while squeezing only n+4 of them out of his brains. We have too high an opinion of our Reader's tastes to irk him with examples of this kind, which are rather common among twentieth century New York pen-wielders; well-known pieces of this type are Peter Meinke's 'Atomic Pantoum' and Robert Hass' 'Pantoum of the Great Depression'.

Pantoums are used in Malay, French and English, usually for melancholy descriptive pieces; it is quite interesting to notice that the word 'pantum' in Malay doesn't indicate any form in particular, and just means 'poem'.

Virelai Ancien

The virelai ancien is likely the most difficult form in *coblas capcaudadas* ever devised. It is made of a sequence of 12-line stanzas. In each of these, lines 1, 2, 4, 5, 7, 8, 10 and 11 rime with each other and have eight metrical syllables, while lines 3, 6, 9, and 12 rime with each other and have four metrical syllables. The pattern is therefore:

AAbAAbAAbAAb

(the lowercased B indicates the shorter verse).

In the next stanza, the longer lines rime with the shorter ones of the *preceding* stanza, while the shorter ones introduce a new rhyme; therefore, the scheme continues as:

AAbAAbAAbAAb BBcBBcBBcBBc

One can go on like that as long as he wishes, but the shorter lines in the last stanza must rime with the longer ones in the first. The Present Author is aware that this is a terrible mess, and sorry he is unable to provide you with any example, as he himself suspects none exists (although Chaucer's virelai is in coblas capifinidas and resembles our definition a bit), and that this metre is merely a speculation. Anyhow, a virelai ancien, e.g., of five stanzas would have this structure:

AAbAAbAAbAAb BBcBBcBBcBBc CCdCCdCCdCCd
DDeDDeDDeDDe EeaEEaEEaEEa

Here is the one piece in all classical English literature that most resembles a virelai ancien:

Alone walkyng
In thought playnyng,
And sore syghyng;
  All desolate,
Me remembryng
Of my lyvyng;
My death wyssyng
  Bothe early and late.

Infortunate
Is so my fate,
That, wote ye what?
  Out of measure
My lyfe I hate;
Thus desperate,
In suche poor estate,
  Doe I endure.

Of other cure
Am I not sure;
Thus to endure
  Is hard, certayn;
Such is my ure,
I you ensure;
What creature
  May have more payn?

My truth so playn
Is taken in vayn,
And grete disdayn
  In remembraunce;
Yet I full fayn
Would me complayne,
Me to abstayne
  From this penaunce.

But, in substaunce,
None alleggeaunce
Of my gryevaunce
  Can I not fynde;
Right so my chance,
Wyth displeasaunce,
Doth me advaunce;
  And thus an ende.

—Geoffrey Chaucer (attributed)

Coblas Unissonantis

Troubadouric Song

The troubadouric song is perfectly alike to an ode, and follows the same rules with one important difference: its stanzas are rhymed as coblas unissonantis rather than as coblas continuadas (refer to the first paragraph), although rhyming also within the same stanza is neither forbidden nor particularly rare. Also, unlike the ode, this metre is almost invariably concluded by an envoi (by a cascade of them, at times), which is built exactly as the other stanzas, but with a number of lines removed starting from the top (the examples will clarify this point better).

The term 'troubadouric song' is appropriate to the most common usage of this form in French and, mostly, Provençal, but it is not standard, and its definition as such is probably exclusive to this guide.

This type of metre was the most popular one among 'trobar clus' Provençal poets around the turn of the twelfth century, but has found applications in French in the same age and in Italian, although very seldom, in the late mediaeval age. The involvement of English in this form was triggered by T. S. Eliot, who shows interest for it in several works; in fact the only explicit English example existing is the second part of the 'Dry Salvages' Quartet, which the Reader is invited to look up. Here are some Neolatin examples:

ANS QUE sim reston de branchas
sec ni despuelhat de fuelha
farai, c'Amors m'o comanda,
breu chanson de razon Ionia,
que gen m'a ducx de las artz de s'escola:
tan sai que'l cors fas restar de suberna
e mos buous es pro plus correns que lebres.

Ab razos coindas et franchas
m'a mandat qu'ieu no m'en tuelha
ni autra no serva ni'n blanda
pus tan fai qu'ab si m'aconia,
e'm ditz que flors no'il semble de viola
que's camja leu si tot noquas iverna,
anz per s'amor sia laurs o genebres.

Ditz "Tu, qu'alhors non t'estanchas
per autra que't denh ni't cuelha;
totz plaitz esquiv'e desmanda
sai e lai qui que't somonia,
que's clama folh qui se meteis afola;
e tu no far falha don hom t'esquerna
mas apres Dieu lieis honors e celebres.

E tu c'o aus, non t'afranchas
per respieg qu'amar no't vuelha:
sec, s'il te fui ni't fai guanda,
que greu er qu'om no'i aponia
qui s'afortis de preiar e no cola,
qu'en passera part las palutz d'Uzerna
Mon Pelegrin lai on cor en jos Ebres."

S'ieu n'ai passatz pons ni planchas
per lieis, cujatz qu'ieu m'en duelha?
Non eu, qu'ab joi es vianda
me sap far mezina conia
baizan tenen, e'l cors, si tot si vola,
no's part de lieis qui'l capdel'e'l governa.
Cors, on qu'ieu an, de lieis no't luins ni't sebres!

De part Nil entro c'a Sanchas
genser no's vest ni's despuelha,
e sa beatatz es tan granda
que semblaria'us messonia;
be'm vai d'Amor, que m'abrassa e m'acola,
e no'm frezis freitz ni gels ni buerna,
ni'm fai doler mals ni gota ni ni febres.

Sieus es Arnautz del sim tro en la sola
e no vuelh ges ses lieis aver Lucerna
ni'l senhoriu del renc per on cort Ebres.
                                    —Arnaut Daniel

Before the tops of the branches become
withered and stripped of leaves
I'll write, since Love commands me so
a short song on a long subject,
since I was taught well the arts of its school:
I know so much that I can stay the running flow
and that my oxen are much quicker than hares.

With words good and fair
she told me not to turn away
nor to serve and flatter anyone else
in the way she likes me so much to do,
and she tells me not to resemble the violet flower,
that changes fast, even when it isn't cold yet,
instead, for her love's sake, to be like laurel or juniper.

She says: "You, care not to settle elsewhere,
with another one that cares for you;
skip and delay all trysts,
whoever and wherever calls you,
because he's a fool who harms himself;
and don't fail so to deserve reproach
but after God, only me celebrate and praise.

And you, who hear, do not free your mind
by telling yourself that she won't love you:
keep on, even if she avoids you and shuns you,
hardly a man can fail his aims
that insists in pleading and does not give up:
such a man would pass safely through the swamps of Uzerne
all the way to the Pilgrim's Mount, where the Ebres runs and jousts."

If I crossed bridges and planks
for her, do you think I complain?
Not I, that out of joy only, without any food,
know how to mix a joyous drug,
kissing and hugging, and my heart, even if it flies,
does not part from her that keeps and rules it.
Heart, wherever I go, don't move nor part from her!

From where the Nile is all the way to Saintes
one more kind does not dress nor undress,
and her beauty is so great
that it would seem false;
Love's good to me, that lets her kiss and hug me,
and nor cold nor ice nor frost can chill me,
nor pain nor disease nor fever makes me ache.

Hers is Arnaut from the head to toe,
and he doesn't want to have, without her, Luzerne
nor the kingdom through which the Ebres flows.

VERDI panni, sanguigni, oscuri o persi
non vestì donna unquanco
né d'or capelli in bionda treccia attorse
sì bella, come questa che mi spoglia
d'arbitrio, e dal camin de libertade
seco mi tira, sì ch'io non sostegno
alcun giogo men grave.

E pur s'arma talor a dolersi
l'anima, a cui vien manco
consiglio, ove 'l martìr l'adduce in forse,
rappella lei da la sfrenata voglia
sùbito vista; ché del cor mi rade
ogni delira impresa, et ogni sdegno
fa 'l veder lei soave.

Di quanto per Amor già mai soffersi,
et aggio a soffrir anco,
fin che mi sani 'l cor colei che 'l morse,
rubella di mercè, che pur l'envoglia,
vendetta fia; sol che contra umiltade
orgoglio et ira il bel passo ond'io vegno
non chiuda e non inchiave.

Ma l'ora e 'l giorno ch'io le luci apersi
nel bel nero e nel bianco
che mi scacciâr di là dove Amor corse,
novella, d'esta vita che m'addoglia,
furon radice, e quella in cui l'etade
nostra si mira, la qual piombo o legno
vedendo è chi non pave.

Lagrima dunque che da gli occhi versi
per quelle, che nel manco
lato mi bagna chi primier s'accorse,
quadrella, dal voler mio non mi svoglia,
ché 'n giusta parte la sentenzia cade:
per lei sospira l'alma; et ella è degno
che le sue piaghe lave.

Da me son fatti i miei pensier diversi:
tal già, qual io mi stanco,
l'amata spada in sé stessa contorse;
né quella prego che però mi scioglia,
ché men son dritte al ciel tutt'altre strade,
e non s'aspira al glorioso regno
certo in più salda nave.

Benigne stelle che compagne fêrsi
al fortunato fianco,
quando 'l bel parto giù nel mondo scorse!
ch'è stella in terra, e come in lauro foglia
conserva verde il pregio d'onestade,
ove non spira folgore né indegno
vento mai che l'aggrave.

So io ben ch'a voler chiuder in versi
suo' laudi fôra stanco
chi più degna la mano a scriver porse:
qual cella è di memoria in cui s'accoglia
quanta vede vertù, quanta beltade,
chi gli occhi mira d'ogni valor segno,
dolce del mio cor chiave?

Quanto il sol gira, Amor più caro pegno,
donna, di voi non have.
—Francesco Petrarca

Green, crimson, dark or azure clothes
never were worn by any woman
neither golden hair was ever twisted in a braid
so beautifully, as does this woman that strips me
of my free will and, away from the path of liberty,
drags me towards herself, so that I can't sustain
any lighter yoke.

However, soul sometimes
takes arms, ready to complain, but the willpower
fails it, when the torment threatens it,
it recalls her, and swerves away from the unholy purpose,
after suddenly envisioning her; away from my heart
every delirious enterprise is razed, and each disdain,
by her suave sight.

No matter how much I have suffered
and still have to suffer,
as long as my heart is healed by her who gnawed it,
merciless, and still tempts it,
I'll be avenged; as long as against humility
her pride and anger don't bar the beautiful path on which I come
and lock it.

But the day and time when I set my eyes
in the white and in the black
that cast me away from where Love ran,
of this new, painful life,
they were the root, and that woman, in which our time
sees itself, if one sees her and doesn't fear her
he must be made of lead or wood.

Oh tear that pour from my eyes,
towards those love-darts
which drench me with blood in the left side
(which was the first to be affected), you do right by me,
the sentence falls on the right part:
it is because of the eyes that the soul sighs; and it is right
that they wash its wounds.

My thoughts sway from me:
somebody already, wretched as I am,
launched her beloved sword against herself;
I don't endear my love to free me
since of all ways, this is the straightest one towards Heaven
and one doesn't aspire to the glorious reign
with a firmer vessel.

Oh goodly stars, that were friendly
to the fortunate loin,
when the beautiful deliverance occurred in the world!
She's a star on Earth and, as the laurel keeps
its foliage green, she maintains her honest worth,
where lightning does not strike neither heinous
wind ever oppresses it.

I know well that attempting to put in verses
her praises would tire
people with hands more gifted for writing:
which memory can hold
all the virtue it sees, all the beauty
one beholds in her eyes, tokens of all worth,
sweet keys of my heart?

No matter how far the sun rides, Love shall never,
woman, have a better pawn than you.

This form was originally devised for courtly love songs, but it has occasionally been employed for lechery, war songs and political themes – almost everything aside from descriptions.

Rime En Kyrielle:

Ballade

A ballade is something akin to an *ode* (in the sense defined earlier in this chapter), but with an *envoi*, and in which the last line of each stanza (envoi included) is the same; points 2 and 3 dictated for the construction of an ode must still be followed, though. As the last line must rhyme with at least another one (see above again), a ballade has, at least partly, a *coblas unissonantis* nature; actually several examples are wholly written in this way. This metre is extremely common in French, and rarer, but still quite popular, in English which, oddly enough, seems to have adopted the most difficult type only. Some examples are here presented:

DOUBLE BALLADE ON THE NOTHINGNESS OF THINGS

The big teetotum twirls
And epochs wax and wane
As chance subsides or swirls;
But of the loss and gain
The sum is always plain.
Read on the mighty pall,
The weed of funeral
That covers praise or blame,
The -isms and the -anities,
Magnificence and shame: —
"O Vanity of Vanities!"

The Fates are subtile girls!
They give us chaff for grain.
And Time, the Thunderer, hurls,
Like bolted death, disdain
At all that heart and brain
Conceive, or great or small,
Upon this earthly ball.
Would you be knight and dame?
Or woo the sweet humanities?
Or illustrate a name?
O Vanity of vanities!

We sound the sea for pearls,
Or drown them in a drain;
We flute it with the merles,
Or tug and sweat and strain;
We grovel, or we reign;
We saunter, or we brawl;
We answer, or we call;
We search the stars for Fame,
Or sink her subterranities;
The legend's still the same: —
"O Vanity of Vanities!"

Here at the wine one birls,
There some one chanks a chain.
The flag that this man furls
That man to float is fain.
Pleasure gives place to pain:
These in the kennel crawl,
While others take the wall.
She has a glorious aim,
He lives for the inanities.
What comes of every claim?
O Vanity of Vanities!

Alike are clods and earls.
For sot, and seer, and swain,
For emperors and for churls,
For antidote and bane,
There is but one refrain:
But one for king and thrall,
For David and for Saul,
For fleet of foot and lame,
For pieties and profanities,
The picture and the frame:—
"O Vanity of Vanities!"

Life is a smoke that curls—
Curls in a flickering skein,
That winds and whisks and whirls,
A figment thin and vain,
Into the vast Inane.
One end for hut and hall!
One end for cell and stall!
Burned in one common flame
Are wisdoms and insanities.
For this alone we came:—
"O Vanity of Vanities!"

Envoi
Prince, pride must have a fall.
What is the worth of all
Your state's supreme urbanities?
Bad at the best's the game.
Well might the Sage exclaim:—
"O Vanity of Vanities!"

       —William Ernest Henley

L'EPITAPHE VILLON

Frères humains qui après nous vivez,
N'ayez les coeurs contre nous endurcis,
Car, si pitié de nous pauvres avez,
Dieu en aura plus tôt de vous mercis.
Vous nous voyez ci attachés cinq, six:
Quant à la chair, que trop avons nourrie,
Elle est piéça dévorée et pourrie,
Et nous, les os, devenons cendre et poudre.
De notre mal personne ne s'en rie;
Mais priez Dieu que tous nous veuille absoudre!

Si frères vous clamons, pas n'en devez
Avoir dédain, quoique fûmes occis
Par justice. Toutefois vous savez
Que tous hommes n'ont pas bon sens rassis;
Excusez-nous, puisque sommes transis,
Envers le fils de la Vierge Marie,
Que sa grâce ne soit pour nous tarie,
Nous préservant de l'infernale foudre.
Nous sommes morts, âme ne nous harie,
Mais priez Dieu que tous nous veuille absoudre!

La pluie nous a débués et lavés,
Et le soleil desséchés et noircis;
Pies, corbeaux, nous ont les yeux cavés,
Et arraché la barbe et les sourcils.
Jamais nul temps nous ne sommes assis;
Puis çà, puis là, comme le vent varie,
À son plaisir sans cesser nous charrie,
Plus becquetés d'oiseaux que dés à coudre.
Ne soyez donc de notre confrérie;
Mais priez Dieu que tous nous veuille absoudre!

Prince Jésus, qui sur tous a maistrie,
Garde qu'Enfer n'ait de nous seigneurie:
À lui n'ayons que faire ni que soudre.
Hommes, ici n'a point de moquerie;
Mais priez Dieu que tous nous veuille absoudre!
                                    —François Villon

Human brothers, who live close to us,
do not harden your heart against us,
since, if you have mercy on our misery,
God will have it sooner on you.
You see us here, hanging, five, six:
as for the flesh, which we have fed too much,
it is wasted, devoured and rotten,
And we, the bones, become ash and dust.
Don't laugh at our mischance;
but pray to God to forgive us all.

If we call you brothers, you ought not
to be wroth, albeit we were killed
out of justice. You know, however,
that common sense is not for everybody;
excuse us, since we have passed away,
to the son of the Virgin Mary,
let not her be devoid of grace towards us,
let her save us from the hellish lightning.
We are dead: let nobody harass us,
but pray to God to forgive us all.

Rain has washed and rinsed us,
the sun has dried and blackened us;
Pies, crows have gauged our eyes,
and torn our beard and eyebrows.
We can't stand still for a second;
here and there, as the wind changes,
it turns us around as it wishes,
more pecked at by birds than thimbles.
Don't be, then, of our kind,
but pray to God to forgive us all.

Prince Jesus, that are the master of everything,
Prevent Hell from ruling over us:
don't let us be indebted towards it.
Men, there is no reason for mockery here;
but pray to God to forgive us all.

D.G. Rossetti's translations of Villon's ballades will present those interested
with more material.

Ballades seem to be fit almost any use, their character being rather determined by the verses chosen for their lines than by the metre in itself.

The earliest examples of this form are found in the fifteenth century, and it still enjoyed some popularity a few decades ago (Eugene o' Neill, and even some pseudo-Celtic folk singers have produced specimens). The influence of ballades ranges beyond proper pieces, and is clearly evident, among many others, in works of George Herbert such as *The Pearl*.

As a note, the French *chant royal*, sometimes regarded as a separate metre, is merely a special type of ballade in coblas unissonantis. The *kyrielle*, from which the name of this section comes, is a type of ballade as well, the most primitive possible one, in which each stanza is made of two rhyming couplets, the second of which always ends with the same line.

Virelai Nouveau

The virelai nouveau is among the rarest metres, and one of the most unclear in its definition; there certainly are French examples, and some authors seem convinced that English and Latin ones exist as well. It only shares the first part of the name with the virelai ancien (see above), and it is even more difficult to write.

This form starts with a couplet, ends with the same (sometimes turned upside-down), and is made of stanzas that use only two rhymes, ending alternately with one of the lines of the starting couplet. Banville's 'Virelai à mes editeurs' is a good example, and Tennyson is said to have written something in this style as well.

This as far as the theory goes; actual virelais generally appear as a disorderly sequences, in which the two rhymes of the first stanza are used alternately in the other ones, and the first line also concludes every even stanza, and the poem.

Of all virelais, the most famous by far is the one by C. de Pisan below, while the short piece concluding Chaucer's *The Parliament of Foules* is perhaps the English examples that most closely resembles the definition above. Of course, as said before, the many English villanelles can also be regarded as virelais nouveaux as well, and this is actually the reason the more general form is described in this treatise, in spite of its obscurity.

JE CHANTE par couverture,
Mais mieux pleurassent mes oeils,
Ni nul ne sait le travail
Que mon pauvre coeur endure.

Pour ce muce ma douleur,
Qu'en nul je ne vois pitié.
Plus a l'on cause de pleur,
Moins trouve l'on d'amitié.

Pour ce plainte ni murmure
Ne fais de mon piteux deuil.
Ainçois ris quand pleurer veuil,
Et sans rime et sans mesure
Je chante par couverture.

Petit porte de valeur
De soi montrer déhaitié,
Ne le tiennent qu'à foleur
Ceux qui ont le coeur haitié.

Si n'ai de démontrer cure
L'intention de mon veuil,
Ains, tout ainsi comme je seuil,
Pour celler ma peine obscure,
Je chante par couverture.
      —Christine de Pisan

I sing to cover it,
but my eyes would rather weep,
no one knows the travail
my poor heart endures.

For this my pain is silent,
because I can't find pity in anyone.
The more reason one has to weep
the less friendship she finds.

For this no complaint nor whisper
I utter about my piteous pain.
Instead I laugh, when I would cry,
and, without rhyme nor reason,
I sing to cover it.

It brings little admiration
to show oneself abated,
they think it's folly,
those whose hearts are exalted.

And if I care not to display
the intention of my will,
instead, such as I use to
to hide my obscure pain,
I sing to cover it.

NOW WELCOM somer, with thy sonne softe,
That hast this wintres weders over-shake,
And driven awey the longe nightes blake!

Saynt Valentyn, that art ful hy on-lofte; -
Thus singen smale foules for thy sake -
Now welcom somer, with thy sonne softe,
That hast this wintres weders over-shake.

Wel han they cause for to gladen ofte,
Sith ech of hem recovered hath his make;
Ful blisful may they singen whan they wake;

Now welcom somer, with thy sonne softe,
That hast this wintres weders over-shake,
And driven away the longe nightes blake.
—G. Chaucer

Glose

A form of Spanish origin, the glose has found acceptance in Central and South America as well, but has never encountered much favour in other linguistic areas. It consists of two parts: a *head* made of a few verses (usually four), often written by someone different from the author of the rest of the piece and a *tail* made of as many stanzas as the lines in the head are. Each stanza is built as a normal ode's, but must end with the corresponding verse of the head: the first stanza ends with the first verse of the head, the second stanza with the second verse and so forth. There is no general rule concerning the construction of the stanzas, except that they must be in coblas continuadas. The rondeau redoublé is, clearly, a variety of this form, so the Voiture piece given in the former chapter should do for a French example; an English and a Spanish one follow:

'A book of verses underneath the bough
a jug of wine, a loaf of bread and thou
beside me singing in the wilderness
oh, wilderness were paradise enough'

OFT have the footsteps of my soul been led
By thee, sweet OMAR, far from hum, of toil
To where the Chenar trees their plumage spread
And tangly vines of wild-grape thickest coil;
Where distant fields scarce glimpst in noon content,
Are lush with verdure quick upon the plough;
Where trull of Nightingale beneath the Tent
Of heaven sinks away to soft lament;
There have I sat with Thee and conned ere now
A book of verses underneath the bough

When from the city's raucous din new-freed
I quaff thy wisdom from the clearing Cup
Of rubáyát, then, even as I read,
I seem with Thee, in Persian groves to sup
On bread of YEZDAKHAST and SHIRAZ Wine
That lifts the net of Care from the brow.
These words, that tongue, the Spirit of the Vine,
Break from the Veil, and lo! the Voice is thine:
Then is my wish - would Fate that wish allow!
A Jug of Wine a Loaf of Bread - and Thou.

Although I tread the Wilderness of life,
Thy song can waft me to that careless clime,
Where enter in nor memories of strife,
Nor ghosts of woe from out of the Gulf of Time.
There, by thy side, great OMAR, would I stray,
And drink the Juice that has forgot the Press,
(A Pot, the Potter shaped but Yesterday -
To-morrow will it be but broken Clay?)
With only Thee the toilsome road to bless,
Beside me singing in the Wilderness.

When Thou dost scorn the waste and mourn the Rose,
That dies upon the world's too sinful breast,
In thy disdain a wondrous beauty glows,
Unfolding visions of a Life more blest.
Then from NAISHAPUR in KHORASAN
I seem to wander, though I know not how,
Within the glittering gates of JENNISTAN,
Supreme SHADUKIAM I wondering scan:
Though still I walk in the Wilderness, I vow -
Oh, Wilderness were Paradise enow!
—Porter Garnett (head by E. Fitzgerald)

'Mientras él mira suspenso
sus bellezas, multiplica
ellas heridas, todas fuertes,
pero ninguna sentida.'
CON LUCIENTE vuelo airoso,

Reina de las aves bellas,
fabrica entre las Estrellas
el ileso nido hermoso.
Mírala el Dragón furioso;
pero, aunque con odio intenso,
mal seguirá el vuelo inmenso
del Águila coronada,
si ella vuela remontada
mientras él mira suspenso.

Mal su anhélito ha intentado
el nido infestar, que ha visto,
porque con la Piedra Cristo
quedó el nido preservado.
Mas ella, al verle burlado,
a Dios el honor aplica;
y cuando, de dones rica,
apocando sus riquezas,
disminuye sus grandezas,
sus bellezas multiplica.

Ave es, que con vuelo grave,
de lo injusto haciendo justo,
pudo hacer a Adán Augusto,
convirtiendo el Eva en Ave.
No el Dragón su astucia alabe:
que si en las comunes muertes
goza victoriosas suertes,
hace en estos lances raros,
é1, todos flacos reparos:
ella, heridas todas fuertes.

¡Qué bien el Ave burló
de sus astucias lo horrendo,
pues su Concepción aun viendo,
su Preservación no vió!
Bien su necedad pensó,
que era el Águila escogida
de su veneno vencida,
aunque miraba, en su daño,
mil señales de su empeño,
Pero ninguna sentida.

—Juana Ines de la Cruz (head by L. de
Góngora)

'While he regards, suspended,
her beauties, she multiplies
those wounds, all deep
but all unawares.'

With a glittering, spirited flight,
Queen of the beautiful birds,
she builds among the stars
the splendid, untouched nest.
The raging Dragon watches her;
but, however intense his hatred is,
he [only] awkwardly follows the immense flight
of the crowned Eagle
if she flies ascending
while he regards, suspended.

Ruefully his yearning has tried to
infest the nest which he has seen,
since by Stone Christ
he left the nest untouched.
But she, seeing him baffled,
honours God instead;
and when, loaded with gifts,
she belittles her riches,
by reducing her greatness
her beauties she multiplies.

It is a bird that, with grave flight,
converting unjust into just,
could make from Adam Augustus,
turning Eve into a bird.
Let not the Dragon boast his guile:
if among the common deaths
he enjoys victorious fortune,
among these rare events
he creates weak lairs only,
she [creates] wounds, all deep.

How well the Bird baffled
the wiles of the Horrid
so that, albeit he saw the Conception,
he couldn't see the Preservation!
Deservingly his foolishness thought
that the chosen Eagle
was won by his venom;
albeit he saw, to his own detriment,
a thousand signs of her constancy
but all unawares.

The glose is still alive and well in South America, and 'Ritmos negros del Perú' a Latino-pop piece by singer Nicomedes Santa Cruz is a perfect example of the form.

'Glosa' roughly means 'explanation' in Spanish, so that this form is practically the long unfolding of a concept contained in the few lines of the head. The character of this poem is then usually religious or philosophical and the opening lines are usually deeply gnomic.

Another variation on the glose (actually, a proper one turned upside-down) is the *sonnet redoublé*, a sequence in which the opening lines of fourteen sonnets are combined, in order, to form a fifteenth one; it was used in Elizabethian times.

Sources and further reading

Although the bibliography given for Chapters I and III covers most topics, troubadouric prosody is not usually talked about in general treatises on modern European poetry, and when it is, rough or erroneous pieces of information are provided. Proper treatises are for specialists and include the unpalatable Billy, D. *L' Architecture lyrique medievale: analyse metrique et modelisation des structures interstrophiques dans la poesie lyrique des troubadours et des trouveres* (Montpellier: Association Internationale d'Etudes Occitanes, 1989) and the ponderous Frank, I. *Répertoire métrique de la poésie des troubadours* (Paris: Champion, 1957), which lists all known rhyme schemes used in Old Provençal. A book the layman can read, and actually enjoy immensely, is Beck, J. *Le melodie dei trovatori secondo la raccolta completa del materiale manoscritto, per la prima volta pubblicato, con l'aggiunta di uno studio sullo sviluppo della notazione musicale (fin verso il 1250) e sul principio metrico-ritmico della poesia lirica medievale, nonché della trascrizione in note moderne delle melodie dei trovadori e trovieri* (Milano: Ulrico Hoepli, 1939); several books by Jean Beck exist in French as well but, quite ironically, his complete works exist only in G. Cesari's Italian translation.

Those interested in how something as remote as Malayan poetry connects with European prosody could read the short article by Brewster, P. G. 'Metrical, Stanzaic and Stylistic Resemblances Between Malayan and Western Poetry.' *Revue de littérature comparée* 32 (1958): 214.

A concise but exhaustive explanation of the coblas theory as applied to mediaeval Italian can be found in Biadene, L. *Il collegamento delle stanze mediante la rima nella canzone dei secoli XIII e XIV.* (Rome: Forzani, 1906).

V Nordic Prosody

This chapter deals with poetic forms used in ancient poems written in Icelandic and other Scandinavian languages; it doesn't aspire to be a complete, comprehensive treatise and it should be regarded mostly as a necessary introduction to the next one. As with the Western European traditions presented before, the point is singling out those aspects of Nordic prosody that have affected the development of English poetry, rather than undertaking the formidable task of producing a satisfactory outline of the techniques used by the skalds over an immense spatial and chronological expanse.

The conventions adopted here are a bit different from those of the former chapters, and a bold letter, or group of letters, will indicate alliterating consonantal sounds rather than a stressed vowel.

Fornyrðislag

This metre, along with málaháttr is the most common in ancient German, Anglo-Saxon and Norse-Icelandic poetry. Fornyrðislag verses have four syllables; the original Germanic metre was not strictly syllable-counting, but followed rules that were distinct from those of verse in the classic and modern languages of Europe. These metres have lived to the present day in Iceland, but have been affected in various ways by developments in pronunciation.

The metre fornyrðislag is known from 700 A.D. in England: *Beowulf* is an example of it. It is also found in German poetry from the eighth century and in Swedish runes from the ninth century. At first, it was rather unclear, but in later poems the form becomes more strict, each stanza having eight lines (in German and English poetry it has four lines).

An example from *Völuspá*:

Hljóðs bið ek allar
helgar kindir
meiri ok minni
mögu Heimdallar
Vildu at ek Valföðr
vel fyr telja
forn spjöll **f**ira
þau **f**remst um man?

—[dystichs 19–22]

Silence I ask from all,
the holy offspring,
greater and lesser
sons of Heimdallr.
Do you wish, Odin,
that I clearly rehearse
of living beings those ancient tales
which I remember from farthest back?

Two lines are connected by alliteration to form pairs:

Vildu at ek Valföðr
Vel fyr telja

This creates the base unit of the metrical structure. In the a-line two words usually alliterate with one word in the b-line.

It can also be just one word in the a-line:

Hljóðs bið ek allar
helgar kindir

But in the b-line readers always find a second non-alliterating syllable to put stress on, matching the second, often alliterating stressed word of the a-line.

Málaháttr

An example of málaháttr taken from Snorri's *Edda*, poem nr. 95:

Munda ek mildingi
þá er Mæra hilmi
flutta-k fjögur kvæði
fimtán stórgjafar
Hvar víti áðr orta
með æðra hætti
mærð of menglötuð
maðr und himins skautum?

When I composed four poems for the king of Norway, he gave
me fifteen enormous presents. Where in the world has a poet
composed such a lofty poem for a king?

Málaháttr is almost the same as fornyrðislag but here the verse has five syllables instead of four. Alliteration connects two lines to form a pair as well:

Hvar viti áðr orta
með æðra **h**ætti

But the form is not necessarily so strict, and it can also have six syllables as here:

Munda ek **m**ildingi
þá er **m**æra hilmi

Or as in this example from *Atlakviða*:

Atli sendi
ár til Gunnars
kunnan segg at ríða
Knéfröðr var sá heitinn

Atli sent
a wise man
riding to Gunnar:
his name was Knéfröðr

It looks like a mixture of fornyrðislag and málaháttr, but in fact this poem is quite old, from year 800 or earlier: in that time, fornyrðislag wasn't that strict. The poet uses shorter line for fast reports, and long lines for explanations.

Fornyrðislag was mostly used for epic poems, but it has something to do with mystery as well; it is mystical and epic. Fornyrðislag has been used in Iceland since the settlers came to Iceland in 870. Examples of fornyrðislag are found in each century. In the eighteenth century poets used it in translating poems by Alexander Pope, Klopstock's *Messiah*, Milton's *Paradise Lost* and so forth. In the beginning of the romantic period, poets used it for their best poems, and even in modern times they still freely employ it.

Kviðuháttr

The kviðuháttr verse form stems from the fornyrðislag, but its structure is stricter: it has 8 lines, like málaháttr and fornyrðislag, but lines number 1, 3, 5 and 7 have only three syllables. An example of it is *Kviðuháttr Sonatorrek* ('Sons' hard revenge') by Egill Skallagrímsson, from which this extract comes:

> Mjök hefr Rán
> **R**yskt um mik
> Emk **of**snauðr at
> **Á**stvinum
> Sleit **m**ar bönd
> Minnar ættar
> Snar þátt af
> **S**jálfum mér

> *The sea took*
> *a treasure from me*
> *I'm poor of*
> *people I love*
> *Ocean broke*
> *my ancestry's ties*
> *a big part*
> *of my own being.*

There are few examples of this form in English. This translation of a romantic poem by Bjarni Thorarensen, *Veturinn* ('Winter') made by Vilhjalmur Stefansson, the Icelandic-American pathfinder, uses it loosely:

> Who rides with such **f**ury
> A **f**iery charger
> Through the **h**igh **h**eavens
> A **h**orse snow-colored?
> The **m**ighty steed
> From his **m**ane tosses
> **F**rozen **f**lakes
> That **f**lutter earthward.

Glowing **g**litters
His **g**ray armor
On his **sh**oulder there hangs
A **sh**ield ice-covered
On his **h**ead he wears
The **h**elm of terror
The **f**earful Aegis
Frosty helmet
He comes from the hoary
Haunts of midnight
Where the world force flows
From the well eternal
Where restless seas
Roar in breakers
On shores without spring
And summerless rocks.
He knows not of age
Though the oldest gods
Where his playmates ere
The earth was fashioned
The last world will die
And desolation
Veil the suns
Ere his way is ended.
The strong are strengthened
When his step approaches
The soft Earth grows firm
In his fierce embraces
The tears she wept
Are turned to diamonds
And her mourning garb
To a mantle of ermine.

'tis not truly said
That when Summer approaches
Winter flees
To the frozen Northland
He broods in the heavens
While humble spring
Leads summer in
Through sunlit meadows
'tis in his hands
The earth turns daily

In his powerful grasp
The poles are twirling
And he leaves
E'en a little moment
Naught of earth
That's near to heaven.
'tis therefore we see
While summer lingers
The mountains still wear
The Winter's livery
'tis therefore we see
That summer melts not
Heaven's hoar-frost
From the head of age.

Ljóðaháttr

The ljóðaháttr stanza typically contains six lines, or two units of three lines each. The first two lines in each unit are connected by alliteration, and the third is also decorated with alliteration. The first two lines have at least two beats and the third three beats.

Examples of this metre are only found in Icelandic; most likely what happened was that in an original quatrain, composed of a-line b-line a-line b-line, the second pair was contracted to provide the third, or 'full', line of the ljóðaháttr unit. It is an extraordinarily supple metre and conveys an archaic impression.

Here is an example from *Hávamál* ('The wisdom of Odin'):

Sá einn **v**eit
er **v**íða ratar
ok hefir **f**jöld um **f**arið
hverju **g**eði
stýrir **g**umna hver
sá er **v**itandi er **v**its.

—[103–108]

He is truly wise
who has travelled far
and knows the ways of the world.
He who has travelled
can tell what spirit
governs the men he meets.

Deyr fé
Deyja frændr
Deyr **s**jálfr ið **s**ama
En **o**rðstír
Deyr **a**ldregi
Hveim er sér **g**óðan **g**etr
—[451–56]

Cattle die
kinsmen die
all men are mortal
words of praise
will never perish
nor a noble name.

The verse doesn't necessarily have four syllables:

Deyr fé
Deyja frændr

('Deyr' carries an independent beat, ad does 'fé')

Charles W. Dunn, Harvard University professor said about the ljóðaháttr:

> The ear is constantly affected by the unpredictable alternations of similarities and dissimilarities; and, because of the freedom of the syllabic count, the placement of the beat in each half-line is also unpredictably varied. One can train oneself to hear such music; and music it is.

Runhenda

Runhenda (runhent metre) is the only ancient metre with an end-rhyme; it is not a defined form in itself, as poets used end-rhyme with other ancient metres, the most common use of runhenda being with fornyrðislag, following an abababab rhyme scheme on the eight-lines metre. This example is by Egill Skallagrímsson who, because of his dwelling in England, brought end-rhyming into Nordic poetry; this is a verse from the poem *Höfuðlausn* (head-ransom) he composed for Eiríkr Bloodaxe in year 950, in York, when Eiríkr was going to chop his head off:

Rauð hilmir hjör
Þar vas hrafna gjör
Fleinn hitti fjör
Flugu dreyrug spjör
Ól flagðs gota
Fárbjóðr Skota
Trað nipt nara
Náttverð ara

The king's sword is red.
There was a raven flock,
a spear meets life,
bloody pikes fly
to feed wolves;
the Scots tell of misfortune
and men gone to hell,
become night-meal for an eagle.

Sources and further reading

We owe the very existence of this chapter to the kindness of Guðmundir
Sigurdsson, who has provided most of the information and examples in a
personal communication. Due to his disappearance, it is hard to provide a
complete bibliography; two books of great interest in the field are Russom,
G. *"Beowulf" and Old Germanic Metre* (Cambridge: Cambridge University
Press, 1998) and Orrick, A. H., ed. *Nordica et Anglica : Studies in Honor of
Stefán Einarsson* (Paris: Mouton, 1968).

VI Alliterative Verse

Anglo-Saxon alliterative verse is basically a more primitive version of the technique used in Nordic poetry and described in the former chapter. Trusting you haven't read it, scared as you were by the ø's, þ's and å's, the Present Author recommends you go back and consult it: it is mostly in English.

A Short History

Alliterative verse was used somewhat properly, and very abundantly, in Old English; it was still used in Middle English, but the 'liberties' granted to the writer then were such that alliteration was little more than a scattered, occasional device in the text, and the rhymed, syllabic forms imported from Southern Europe by Chaucer and others soon overcame its last remnants.

As 'national identity' became a factor in the Romantic age and British poets began to cherish the idea they hadn't spent the middle ages living in caves and eating acorns, some of them, among which Coleridge, attempted what they fancied to be alliterative verses, producing none, but creating some interesting pieces nonetheless. Lastly, in the recently dead twentieth century, such poets as Ted Hughes and Ezra Pound have resumed writing pieces more or less as in the old times, and that's just as good as poetry gets today.

Alliteration (Definition)

Whatever your favourite dictionary might say about the matter, alliteration in ancient Nordic and English poetry is a correlation between two words defined as the identity of the first sounds preceding the vowel(s) in the syllables carrying the primary stresses. Examples are 'but-tocks' and 'bran-ding' or 'sod-o-mise' and 'con-cern'. Also, in most works of this type, this definition is valid if there is no such sound, as in the 'arse' and 'hon-est' couple.

Nitpickers should be reminded that a word usually has only *one* primary stress, so that the definition lends itself to no ambiguity.

Versification Based on Beats

This technique is a commonly mentioned myth in modern poetry, but it was actually used in alliterative verse, and (with some further restrictions, the topic shan't be touched here) in classic Latin poetry. Its origin is extremely old, as it was already used in the Middle East in the twentieth century B.C., and perhaps even earlier. It is the only alternative to syllabic count practised before free verse, and therefore it deserves some respect; it consists in writing verses which have a fixed number of clearly perceivable main stresses, and the true problem in writing them is making their nature and position unmistakable.

A major drawback of this otherwise brilliant metric idea is that a sequence of lines written in this way, and with the same beats count, tends to sound as dull as a Swiss Sunday. Blake often appears to resort to this technique to try to give some unity to his (slightly) unruly verses. It is, in this Author's opinion, just a coincidence. There is, however, purpose in 'A Crocodile' by Thomas Lovell Beddoes (next time you wonder 'what's in a name?', think of this one):

> HARD by the lilied Nile I saw
> A duskish river-dragon stretched along,
> The brown habergeon of his limbs enamelled
> With sanguine almandines and rainy pearl:
> And on his back there lay a young one sleeping,
> No bigger than a mouse; with eyes like beads,
> And a small fragment of its speckled egg
> Remaining on its harmless, pulpy snout;
> A thing to laugh at, as it gaped to catch
> The baulking merry flies. In the iron jaws
> Of the great devil-beast, like a pale soul
> Fluttering in rocky hell, lightsomely flew
> A snowy trochilus, with roseate beak
> Tearing the hairy leeches from his throat

(this example has four stresses per line, for the most distracted among the Readers).

The Alliterative Verse

The origin of alliterative verse would be obvious to anyone that:

- has read Chapter VI of this manual

- has noticed how Swedes, Danes, Icelanders and Norses read
  Old English with much more ease than any native Englishman

- realises that line breaks had no importance in ancient poetry

As these conditions are not verified simultaneously in any being on Earth except for the Present Author, He shall enlighten you on the point. Take, for example, the fornyrðislag: if two verses of this form are crammed in the same line, the result is a single verse with two beats before a caesura and two beats after it; moreover, alliteration (in the sense defined above) will connect the first three stress-bearing words. That is exactly how alliterative verse is built in Old English. An example is the first of the Exeter riddles (which the Present Author cannot even read, imagine solve, but which illustrates the point nicely):

Hwylc is **hæ**le**þ**a þæs **h**orsc | ond þæs **h**ygecræftig
þæt þæt **m**æge asecgan, | hwa **m**ec on sið wræce,
þonne ic a**st**ige **st**rong, | **st**undum reþe,
þrymful **þ**unie, | **þ**ragum wræce
fere geond **f**oldan, | **f**olcsalo bærne,
ræced **r**eafige? | **R**ecas stigað,
haswe ofer **h**rofum. | **H**lin bið on eorþan,
wælcwealm **w**era, | þonne ic **w**udu hrere,
bearwas **b**ledhwate, | **b**eamas fylle,
holme ge**h**refed, | **h**eahum meahtum
wrecen on wa**þ**e, | **w**ide sended;
hæbbe me on **h**rycge | þæt ær **h**adas wreah
foldbuendra, | **f**læsc ond gæstas,
somod on **s**unde. | **S**aga hwa mec þecce,
oþþe **h**u ic **h**atte, | þe þa **h**læst bere.

Those in search of further examples can browse the Georgetown University Old English database (see below) to their heart's content.

The piece reported:

- fits in the fornyrðislag formerly described

- is incomprehensible to humans Copenhagen's north of

- has lines that can be split in two without loss of 'poetic identi-
  ty' or whatever other virtue Farmer Joe attributes to line breaks
  when preparing his diary for the publisher.

Asking to adhere to such a strict form century after century of a popula-
tion which, for the most part, *did* actually feed on acorns and live in caves,
however, seemed to be impossible, and the readers with the keenest eyes will
have probably noticed some of the lines of the Exeter riddle do not comply
fully to the metre as it is described. The first thing to be removed from the
complete aa|ax idea (where letters now denote alliterations rather than rhym-
ing as in chapters 2–5) was the fact that *all* the first three beats should be
preceded by alliterating sounds: in *Beowulf* and other longish sagas, the rule
is slackened and the first beat of the second hemistich has to alliteratively
match only *one* of those of the first, practically leading to three possibilities:

- aa|ax

- ay|ax

- ya|ax

Later Involution

After the transition from Old English to the actually readable Middle
English, the metres we are concerned with here begin to be used for longer
works, and in an even more relaxed way. The number of beats can indiffer-
ently be four or five (in the latter case the caesura, still mandatory, falls after
the third beat) and the patterns of alliteration within the verse offer many
more choices than before, including ones that involve separate alliterative
groups within the same line. A list, probably incomplete, could be this:

- Traditional: aa|ax

    Clannesse who-so **k**yndly **c**owthe comende (Cleanness)

- Overdone: aa|aa

In a somer seson, when softe was the sonne
(Piers Plowman)

- Augmented (obtained by cramming one more beat in the scheme):

  — Alliterating: aaa|ax

  On **r**ode **r**wly to**r**ent with **r**ybaudes mony (Patience)

  — Non alliterating: aay|ax

  Kynde hath **c**losed therinne **c**raftily withalle
  (Piers Plowman)

- The last two together (overdone and augmented): aaa|aa

  And **l**ene thee **l**ede thi **l**ond so **l**eaute thee **l**ovye
  (Piers Plowman)

- With a switch: aa|xa

  And **h**even my **h**appe and al my **h**ele (Pearl)

- Plainly screwed up: aa|bb

  To **p**ay the **P**rince other **s**ete **s**aghte (Pearl)

- Screwed up and prolonged: aaa|bb

  And bi**s**egede, **s**oothly, with **s**evene **g**rete **g**eaunts
  (Piers Plowman)

- (Lo and behold) Screwed twice: ab|ab

  And whoso **b**ummed there**o**f, he **b**oughte it ther**a**fter
  (Piers Plowman)

Actually, the situation was not so tragic as it might seem, and most of the structures above are quite rare in comparison to the traditional ones, but the seed of anarchy, in a sense, was cast. In addition to that, an increasing interest turned, in the age of Middle English, towards the *end of the verse*: Langland's *Piers Plowman* only has feminine lines, while the anonymous *Pearl* is heavily rimed: the end of alliterative verse, as king Herod's, came from its toes.

Sources and further reading

Even the staunch scholars that love books and their dust (and the Present Author is one of their number) ought, at times, to make concessions to modernity: there is little doubt that an invaluable source for the study of Old English poetry is the Georgetown University Old English database, found on the World Wide Web at the address *http://www.georgetown.edu/labyrinth/library/oe/alpha.html*. Unlike most pages of this kind, this one, at least in the moment these notes are being written, can be consulted for free by everyone.

Of course, a number of good texts on the subject exist as well, including the clear, concise Schmidt, A.V.C. *The Clerkly Maker: Langland's Poetic Art* (Cambridge: Cambridge University Press, 1987), Dunn, C. W., and Byrnes, E. T., ed., *Middle English Literature* (New York: Garland Publishing, 1990), also quoted in the former chapter, and the innovative, fascinating Toswell, M. J., ed. *Prosody and Poetics in the Early Middle Ages. Essays in Honour of C.B. Hieatt* (Toronto: University of Toronto Press, 1995). The latest representative of the school that thinks *all* English verse is alliterative is the opinionated, synthetic Roberts, P. *How Poetry Works* (Penguin: Harmondsworth, 2000) which, among many, sometimes purposeful, misconceptions, underlines some very interesting points.

VII Phonetic Rhetoric and Advanced Poetic Devices

The last part of this treatise will guide the Reader through some of the techniques that make a piece sound poetic in addition to those described in former chapters; one can think of using these to *substitute* them, thus moving towards actual free verse (as opposed to the prosaic rambling that is often defined as such). This chapter will, in fact, be the first one displaying examples of it.

It is essential, in reading what follows, that one be not scared by the abundance of Greek names: they are all fully explained, while even the Author, for all His magnificence, doth not remember them all by heart himself.

What is Phonetic Rhetoric

Strictly speaking, rhetoric in general is simply the set of all techniques used in making language more effective. Most, if not all, of these techniques, therefore, can affect poetry and, before these sad times of teen angst, pop lyrics, rural journals, gothic onanists, ethnic masters, 'creative writing' majors and plain fools, poetry was the human activity that teemed the most with them.

However, this guide is committed to treating only the phonetic aspects of the subject, and must therefore cut a distinction between those rhetorical techniques, such as the figures of speech, the nature of which is entirely conceptual, and those, like the anaphora, which have at least a partial phonetic nature.

The brightest Readers will have, by this point, have inferred that a good part of the essence of poesy involves phonetic repetition: repetition of syllabic patterns in Chapter I, repetition of verse endings in Chapter II, of entire lines in Chapter III, of stanza structures in Chapter IV, of alliterating consonants in chapters V and VI. It is now time for us to consider repetition in a less systematic way as a rhetoric tool. The first, and most elementary, technique is quite obvious.

Iteratio (Repetition of Words or of Groups)

This is by far the most abused, but at the same time the subtlest technique, which groups several well-known devices. The most basic one is called *geminatio*, consisting in plainly saying the same thing twice in a row, as in these examples:

> Tyger! Tyger! burning bright
> In the forests of the night (Blake)

> César, calme César, le pied sur toute chose [a] (Valéry)

(the adjective 'calme' doesn't carry any stress for most readers and doesn't really change the effect of immediate reiteration).

All in all, geminatio seems to be good for one thing only, that is, placing more emphasis on a vocative; it gives a poem some resemblance to a lullaby, and is, generally speaking, a remarkably silly device. But Valéry's 'César' is a masterpiece, and its character depends much on it; so, at least, some good can come from it.

A more common, and more seriously used (and, very often, misused) device is the anaphora, consisting in the repetition of the same word or group at the beginning of each logical structure; this structure can be a verse:

> PER ME SI VA NELLA CITTÀ DOLENTE,
> PER ME SI VA NELL'ETTERNO DOLORE,
> PER ME SI VA TRA LA PERDUTA GENTE
> —Dante

> *Through me one goes to the painful city*
> *Through me one goes to eternal pain*
> *Through me one goes to the lost people*

> Je congnois bien mouche en lait
> Je congnois a la robe l'homme
> Je congnois le beau temp du let
> Je congnois au pommier la pomme
> —Villon

I know well the fly in the milk
I know a man by his clothes
I know the Golden Age of milk
I know the tree by the apple

(entire poems have been written anaphorically this way, e.g., Cecco Angi-
olieri's 'S'io fossi foco', Villon's 'Ballade des menus propos', to which the
fragment above belongs, 'Ballade des contre verites' and 'Ballade des prover-
bes', Peire Cardenal's 'Ar me puesc ieu lauzar d'Amor', Blake's 'An Ancient
Proverb') or it can be a stanza:

HESPERUS the day is gone
Soft falls the silent dew
A tear is now on many a flower
And heaven lives in you

Hesperus the evening mild
Falls round us soft and sweet
'Tis like the breathings of a child
When day and evening meet

Hesperus the closing flower
Sleeps on the dewy ground
While dew falls in a silent shower
And heaven breathes around

Hesperus thy twinkling ray
Beams in the blue of heaven
And tells the traveller on his way
That earth shall be forgiven
—John Clare

Anaphoras are sometime used on a larger (every several stanzas) or smaller
(within hemistichs) scale, and in classic poetry they serve the purpose of
stiffening the structure, giving the verses a gnomic, prophetic or plainly
insistent character, that sometimes suits humorous compositions. Anaphora
is employed differently in free verse, where it co-ordinates its various parts in
what one may term pseudo-stanzas; this usage is very common in twentieth
century Spanish poetry (see for example García Lorca's 'La sangre derrama-
da', Rafael Alberti's 'Invitación a l'aire', Antonio Machado's 'Anoche cu-
ando dormía') but is found in other languages as well, such as in Italian (see
Montale's Madrigale XV, Clemente Rebora's 'O poesia, nel lucido verso')
and English (see Pound's Canto XLV, under the Present Author's guaran-

tee that it isn't remotely as irksome as the rest of the monumental, tedious, pretentious work in which it is set).

This way of using anaphoras derives from the form of religious hymns, in which a verse or couplet precedes an ample interval of free rambling, and its popularity in Spain should not, therefore, come as a surprise. Many structured poems have been built in this style (a fixed couplet followed by a regular stanza), for example, by Baudelaire, Apollinaire, Laforgue, Rimbaud, Keats and, especially, Tennyson. This chant-like structure, if the opening part is too long or pompous (as is almost always the case) tends to make poems sound stuffy and oppressive. Even masters like Apollinaire generally manage to annoy their readers with it, and the Present Author declines any responsibility if anyone attempting to employ it gets lynched by an angry audience.

Anaphoras, especially those at the beginning of stanzas, are often slightly varied from one instance to the other, or used in two alternating groups. The most remarkable occurrence of the latter case is in the Provençal (but there are plenty of Italian and French examples as well) Contrast, in which each stanza begins with a vocative, as you can see, e.g., in Raimbaut de Vaqueiras' 'Domna, tant vos ai preiada'.

Similar to the anaphora and geminatio, but rarer than either, are *epanalepsis* (reiteration of a word or group in the middle of a structure) and *epanadiplosis* (use of the same word or group both at the beginning and at the end of a structure); the former is rather typical in Ludovico Ariosto, the latter quite rare in poetry. Both are used to stress the importance of a particular sound (or concept), usually by using it with different meanings. A somewhat irritating use of these techniques is the pun, something one would imagine only to belong to humour, but which some celebrated authors employ profusely in a poetic context. These two examples, both by Seamus Heaney, illustrate both devices thus applied:

> Perch [the fish] on their water-perch hung in the clear Bann River
> Stable [noun] child grown stabler

Less deleterious cases do, of course, exist in all Western European languages.

Of course, not all occurrences of geminatio fall into one of the sub-categories above: sometimes words (or separate sounds) are repeated in distant parts of a poem or stanza with the purpose of highlighting them as 'keywords' of sorts. An English example of this can be found in Chapter VIII, and an even clearer one is provided by Apollinaire:

LES COLCHIQUES

Le **pré** est vénéneux mais joli en **automne**
Les **vaches** y paissant
Lentement s'empoissonnent
Le **colchique couleur** de **cerne** et de lilas
Y **fleurit** tes **yeux** sont comme cette **fleur**-là
Violâtres comme leur cerne et comme cet **automne**
Et ma vie pour tes **yeux lentement s'empoisonne**

Les enfants de l'école viennent avec fracas
Vêtus de hoquetons et jouant de l'harmonica
Ils cueillent les **colchiques** qui sont comme des mères
Filles de leurs **filles** et sont couleur de tes paupières
Qui **battent** comme les **fleurs battent** au vent dément

Le gardien du troupeau chante tout doucement
Tandis que lentes et meuglant les **vaches** abbandonnent
Pour toujours ce grand **pré** mal **fleuri** par l'**automne**.

SAFFRONS

The lawn is poisonous but pretty in autumn
The cows, passing there,
Slowly poison themselves
The saffron, colour of circle and lilacs
Blooms there your eyes are like that flower
Purplish as their circle and as this autumn
And my life, for your eyes, slowly poisons itself

The children out of the school come noisily
Dressed in hiccups and playing the harmonica
They pluck the saffrons which are like mothers
Daughters of their daughter and they're the colour of your eyelids
Which flutter like the flowers flutter in the demented wind

The herdsman sings quite sweetly
while slow and lowing the cows abandon
forever that big lawn badly flowered by Autumn

To conclude, one should take note that, obviously, identity rhyme can be seen as a form of geminatio as well: refer to Chapter II for examples.

Homoeoprophoron

This god-awful word is used by Lausberg to indicate the repetition of consonants or syllables at a short distance; in *prose* it is a defect, he hastens to add. In poetry it is a fundamental technique; however, it is necessary to use the term a bit more broadly, and include in it the repetition of vowels. It is true that in European languages there is a stricter sign/sound correlation when it comes to consonants, that the border separating between different vowel sounds tends to be a bit blurred (and to change with time) and that consonants are more or less the same in all languages (while vowels even change from town to town, or from social group to social group within England itself), so that homoeoprophoron *is* actually mostly a consonantal matter.

The repetition of the same sound or group is not very different, as far as the effect goes, to that of the same word: the usage of the same syllable consonant twice in a row, for example, in analogy to the geminatio (see above) produces childish words just as much as geminatio produces childish lines. It is almost universal that 'basic' words, the few that penetrate the under-developed brain of a new-born child, e.g., 'baby', 'papa', 'mum', are centred on this basic use of homoeoprophoron; keeping this fact in mind, other words related to infancy, such as 'lull' are built in the same way. The 'argot' of French youth, the purpose of which is oftentimes to make the speaker sound like a proper fool, is rife as well with words like 'zozou' and 'dodo', while there is a widespread habit among some second-generation rich in Italy of calling each other nicks like 'Tati' and 'Giangi' as a token that they don't need to exercise their brains to survive. As a consequence, even words like 'vivid' might sound a bit silly by association, and proper poets usually try to avoid them as much as possible.

It is instead fairly common in poetry that the same few sounds are repeated several times across a couple or more lines, to give them a sort of unity; this usage is the sound equivalent of the anaphora (see above) and is found in many examples, some of which strikingly famous. Milton uses this device almost obsessively in his *Paradise Lost* as something of a replacement of rime in joining couples of lines, e.g.:

Of man's first disobedience and the fruit
Of that forbidden tree, whose mortal taste
Brought death into the world and all our woe,
With loss of Eden till one greater Man
Restore us and regain the blissful seat
Sing, Heav'nly Muse, that on the secret top
Of Oreb, or of Sinai, didst inspire...
—[1.1–7]

(other homoeoprophora are present than those indicated, which are only the most obvious ones).

Dante often conjoins this device with cacophonic writing (see next chapter) as here:

Perch'io parti' così giunte persone
Partito porto il mio cerebro, lasso!,
dal suo principio ch'è in questo troncone.
Così s'osserva in me lo contrappasso
—[If., 28.136–140]

Since I parted such close persons,
I carry my brain, alas, detached
from its root, which is in this stump.
One can see such reprisal on me.

(quite masterly, Dante reiterates the **[r]** sound, one of the harshest in the Italian language, passing from a **<p + r>** to an **<r + t>** group).

It should be quite apparent now that several well-known poetic devices, as well as a countless multitude of others that theoreticians of rhetoric and language 'discover' from time to time are nothing but sub-varieties of homoeo-prophoron. We shall not even try to enumerate them all but, as a general rule, let the Reader keep in mind that in order to make the reiteration of a sound be more clearly perceived, one ought to either create a number of close occurrences of it, or highlight it in some other way; phonetic ways of doing so include clustering several repeated sounds (thus creating the mid-verse rhyme, assonance and consonance) or placing them in a set position in the word, for example at the beginning or before the main stress (thus creating alliteration, which itself is often confused with homoeoprophoron).

Paragram

A much more subtle application, that only a handful of extremely skilled poets have used, is that of the paragram, or distribution of sounds over a length of text (technically speaking, a paragram is a different thing; we'll use the term here in the sense defined by de Saussurre, however, and stick to it). This device has been theoretically recognised for the first time by de Saussurre in analysing Baudelaire's *Spleen* series: the first three poems, out of four, contain the PL group in the first line:

Pluviôse, irrité contre la ville entière [b] (Spleen I)

J'ai **pl**us de **s**ouvenirs que si j'avais mille ans [c] (Spleen II)

Je **s**uis comme le roi d'un pays **pl**uvieux [d] (Spleen III)

But it is the *fourth* of the series, which de Saussurre overlooked, that, in the *second* line, gives the clearest key to this technique:

Quand le ciel bas e lourd pèse comme un couvercle
Sur l'esprit gémi**ss**ant en **p**roie aux **l**ongs en**n**uis [e]

Here, with adamantine clarity, the consonants preceding the last four stresses of the verse form the sounds SPLN (the sound of the English group *ee*, [i:] according to the I.P.A., does not exist in French, in spite of what a multitude of tin-eared travellers might think about the matter).

Of course, not all examples of paragrammatic writing are so clear; paragrams almost always go together with *anagrams*; as far as the latter are concerned, it is necessary to notice that the traditional anagram one uses in Scrabble games (which merely consist in rearranging letters), due to the imperfect match between sign and sound in European alphabets, is *not* the kind used in poetry: e.g., 'lead' [**lɛd**] (the metal), phonetically, is not an anagram of 'deal' [**di:l**], but rather of 'dell' [**dɛl**] (the square brackets show the International Phonetic Alphabet notations, which illustrate the point nicely to those able to read them; any English dictionary, except for Webster, can shed light on them).

Explicit examples of this transformation are given by Prévert:

Ah **mes salauds**, c'est **Salomé** [f]

Paragrams were not invented by Baudelaire: the same technique is used in much older examples, and with the same purposes, that is, giving unity to a piece, or to part of it, by disseminating some keywords throughout its length. The same authors quoted above when describing the plain homoeoprophoron, often apply the paragram: Dante, when introducing some key characters in the *Inferno*, sometimes uses this device to make them more memorable:

> O **Simon Mago**, **o mi**seri seguaci
> —[19.1]

O Simon the Magician! O miserable followers!

> rimembriti di **Pier da Medicina**
> se mai torni a veder lo dolce **pi**ano
> che **da** Verce**l**li a **M**arcabò **dichi**na.
> —[28.73–75]

Remember Pier da Medicina
if you ever go back and see the sweet plains
sloping from Vercelli to Marzabò

(this example can be read with a different, weaker paragrammatic key, we leave that to the Reader as an exercise).

England, ever richer in playwrights than in poets, has no Dante to boast, no Baudelaire, and therefore very few paragrams. One, very weak in truth, is found, and somewhat declared, in Keats:

> Therefore 'tis with full happiness that I
> Will trace the story of **Endymion**.
> The v**ery** **m**usic **o**f the **n**ame has **g**one
> —[1.34–36]

(The omission of the sounds ND is perhaps purposeful: there is little music in it. It would, however, be a little too flattering to presume such subtlety from a stuffed shirt like Keats; so let the Reader decide whether it was purposeful or he just couldn't find any way of cramming those two sounds in). The most obvious and primitive (due, again, to the imperfect sound-sign correspondence) form of paragram is the acrostic; Villon uses it in the envoi of several ballades to sign them:

Voulez vous que verté vous die?
Il n'est jouer qu'en maladie,
Lettre vraye que tragedie,
Lasche homme que chevalereux,
Orrible son que melodie,
Ne bien conseillé qu'amoureux.

Should I tell you the truth?
There is no joy but in ill health
no truth that isn't drama
no vile man that isn't a knight
no horrible sound that isn't melody
no well-advised man who isn't a lover.

Again, Keats provides the interested Reader with an explicit, although imperfect, example in his poem 'An acrostic'.

Lipogram

The realisation of a phonetic effect in poetry is not achieved only by accumulating similar sounds but also by systematically removing others that could be used. This procedure has a long tradition in poetry; the term *lipogram* was first applied by Salomon Certon in the early seventeenth century. Explicit examples of lipogram exist practically only in French: a few one-vowel poems have been written in Italian, but they are more an academic game than an attempt at artistic expression. Here is a sonnet that does not use the letter E, therefore ruling out at least four distinct sounds of the French language ([e], [ø] and [œ] according to the *I.P.A.*, as well as the schwa), written by Certon himself:

Pour ravir la toison quand Jason courut tant,
Il y parvint pour vray, l'arrachant hors du sort
Aux dragons flamboyans: mais non par son bras fort,
Non par son bac fatal à Cholsos loing flottant.

Car sans ton fort pouvoir qui luy fut assistant
O doux fils à la nuict, par un subtil confort,
Son cas alloit fort mal; il y fust plustost mort,
Tant grand, tant bon fust-il, tant hardy combattant.

Mais tu luy fus amy, quand ton appas charmoit
Son dragon, qui sans fin son tison allumoit,
Il joüit donc par toy du prix ainsi conquis

Donc à toy qui luy fis un tant amy support,
Un tour tant à propos, un tant divin confort,
Soit un los immortal a tout jamais acquis.

When Jason travelled so much to steal the fleece
he obtained it, indeed, snatching it against all odds
from flaming dragons; but it wasn't because of his strong arm
nor because of that fateful ship floating for such a long time at Cholos.

Since, without your might (which assisted him,
o sweet daughter of the night, with a subtle help)
his case would have been an ill one, he would likely have died
no matter how strong, how good, how valiant he was

But you were his friend, when your charm appeased
his dragon, whose torch burnt without end:
he enjoyed then, because of you, the prize won so

It is to you, then, who were such a friendly support for him,
such a lucky chance, such a divine aid
that goes an immortal praise you never acquired.

Beyond the scarcity and obscurity of its 'pure' applications, the lipogram
still is an extremely important archetype in poetry: an example of this is the
care with which French poets before Baudelaire tried to avoid the use of
nasal vowels, which hinder the fluency of reading. The importance of lipo-
grammatic writing is keyed to the fact that the introduction of cacophonic
sounds in a euphonic poem, or vice-versa, weakens or utterly spoils its effect,
and as such it will only be fully understood in the next chapter. However, li-
pograms can be used to create a contrast between different parts of a poem,
whose separation is accentuated by the different set of sounds. The same
lines by Dante used above to illustrate the homoeoprophoron provide a nice
example:

Perch'io parti' così giunte persone
Partito porto il mio cerebro, lasso!,

The word 'lasso', breaks a lipogram in which the letters L and A were kept
at a minimum in order to promote the hard-plodding movement of the Rs;

'lasso' being an exclamation, its smooth-flowing sound comes as a sort of shock to the reader, realising exactly the desired effect.

The simplest way of creating a contrast, and European poets realised this as far back as in the twelfth century, is using different languages: since hardly two languages contain the same set of sounds, the creation of two separate lipogrammatic groups is automatically granted. This usage of multilingual writing creates a sensation of sharp contrast, and it is in the Provençal form of the discord that it was first used in European poetry. A masterful example by Raimbaut de Vaqueiras ('Eras quan vey verdeyar') is still known, and is the beacon of the genre; here is its envoi, which uses Provençal, Italian, French, Gascon and Galician, in this order, for two lines each.

> Belhs Cavaliers, tant es car
> Lo vostr' onratz senhoratges
> Que cada jorno m'esglaio.
> Oi me lasso que farò
> Si sele que j'ai plus chiere
> Me tue, ne sai por quoi
> Ma dauna, he que dey bos
> Ni peu cap santa Quitera,
> Mon corasso m'avetz treito
> E mot gen favlan furtado.

> *Beautiful knight, so dear it is to me*
> *your honoured dominion*
> *that I wither each day*
> *Alas, what shall I do*
> *If the one I hold the dearest*
> *kills me (I don't know why)?*
> *My lady, that which I owe you*
> *Saint Quitera can't atone*
> *You have betrayed my heart,*
> *stolen by many people's slandering.*

With the same spirit, multilingual writing is used by Pound in several of his *Cantos* (in others it is used merely as a vulgar display of knowledge, which is common but nonetheless pathetic) e.g., in the already mentioned Canto XLV, where the mix of French, Italian and Dutch names portrays the wide-spread damages of the practice of usury; it is used by Eliot as well, when the many loose voices at the end of the *Wasteland* overlap each other in different languages to give an impression of the folly (he seems to strongly disagree with the late K. Marx on this point) of the multitudes. The general effect is semantically reinforced by the fact that they say things that have very little in common:

> Shall I at least set my lands in order?
> London Bridge is falling down, falling down, falling down
> Poi s'ascose nel foco che gli affina
> Quando fiam uti chelidon — O swallow, swallow
> La prince d'Aquitaine à la tour abolie
> These fragments I have shored against my ruin
> Why then Ile fit you. Hyeronimo's mad againe
> Datta. Dayadhvam. Damyata.
> Shantih shantih shantih
> 　　　　　　　　—[lines 425–433]

Langland (following an established tradition in mediaeval literature) uses a similar technique in a more orderly and systematic way in *Piers Plowman*: Latin sentences are mixed with English ones to express divine edicts or angelic voices, thus phonetically enforcing the idea that those sentences are beyond the scope of a degenerate mankind.

Multilingual writing is therefore a way of highlighting the different 'personalities' acting in a piece, thus turning it, in a sense, into a one-man play. Its origin dates to the part of the Middle Ages during which poetry lost its musical connotations, and the monotony of single human speech created a vast number of pieces based on imaginary dialogs. The error Pound so often incurs, using different tongues for the sole purpose of boasting, which is rather common among modern poetasters as well, inevitably makes them sound like they're deeply schizophrenic, rather than deeply learned.

Multilingual writing can, and has been, used also in an attempt to expand the phonetic possibilities of a language; in this case the different languages are not used in separate lines, but blended together. Parnasse poet Louis Bouilhet was perhaps the most obdurate pursuer of this aim, studying Chinese for years for this sole purpose. It is possible that he has succeeded splendidly: the present Author, not knowing any Chinese himself, is completely unable to tell. If the Reader is acquainted with oriental languages, he might appreciate this opening quatrain of a piece of his:

La fleur Ing-wha, petite et pourtant des plus belles
n'ouvre qu'à Ching-tu-fu son calice odorant;
et l'oiseau Tung-whang-fung est tout juste assez grand
pour couvrir cette fleur en tendant ses deux ailes

The Ing-wha flower, small and therefore among the jolliest,
Only opens its perfumed chalice during Ching-tu-fu
And the Tung-whang-fung bird is just large enough
to cover that flower by stretching its two wings

Again, should one throw the odd foreign word in a poem just to show
people that he knows it, rather than learned he would sound delirious.

Sources and further reading

The seminal work in which the concept of paragram is illustrated is de Saussure, F. *Cours de linguistique générale* (Paris: Payot, 1995). A work dealing with the various aspects of rhetoric in general is Lausberg, H. *Elemente der literarischen Rhetorik* (München: Max Hueber Verlag, 1967); *Linguistica romanza. I fonetica* (Milano: Feltrinelli, 1971) by the same author is also an interesting reading as it treats in detail the differences among the several Romance languages. In the same field, Jakobson, R., and Waugh L. R. *The Sound and Shape of Language* (Bloomington: Indiana University Press, 1979) provides a deep insight in infantile speech.

Specialised treatises, whose reading is somewhat more difficult but very rewarding, include Contini, G. *Varianti e altra linguistica* (Torino: Einaudi, 1970); Del Monte, A. *Retorica, stilistica e versificazione* (Torino: Loescher, 1981); Barilli, R. *Poetica e retorica* (Milano: Mursia, 1969) Delas, D., and Filliolet, J. *Linguistique et poétique* (Paris: Larousse, 1973).

Morier, H. *Dictionnaire de poétique et de rhétorique* (Paris: Presses Universitaire de France) is exhaustive and interesting, but known to contain some errors, the Reader should, therefore, approach it with some caution.

Those interested in the aspect of Langland's poetry mentioned in this chapter might find Alford, J. 'The Role of the Quotations in Piers Plowman', *Spec.* 52 (1977): 80–99 an alluring reading.

VIII Sound Effects

Up to this point, this guide has only addressed the issue of how *random* sounds are arranged in a poetic way. We have, in fact, systematically ignored the problem of *which* sounds, among the many a language contains, should be used. It is some consolation that we have shared this beastly attitude with pretty much all prosodists up until the present day, who either ignore the subject entirely or just mention that there are 'euphony' (poems that sound good) and 'cacophony' (poems that sound bad, like their author sat down and decided to write a piece of rubbish just for the sake of it).

Facing this topic would be a fairly simple task if we were only considering English; but given the fact that we are trying to show its relationship with other Western European languages, things are bound to become a little confusing. The Present Author apologises in advance and, for clarity's sake, he will do what he seldom does: start from the beginning, of humanity.

The Onomatopoeic Nature of Language

When the first caveman tried to inform his comrades of the presence of a bird in the vicinity, he probably pointed; this almost certainly failed, as some of his associates, thinking he was indicating a woolly mammoth, probably fled. He then, most likely, tried flapping his hands, and this worked, but, as his club fell from his grip, ravaging several of his toes and preventing him from further pursuing the tasty member of the local ornis, he shouted and considered using his mouth instead. So, on later occasions, he most likely chirruped. In the course of these few hundreds of thousands of years, the invention of grammar and several other factors, the nature of which would exceed both the scope of this work and the Reader's patience, have mutated language (though several words, such as 'chirrup', are still clearly recognisable as being of imitative origin): sound is no longer used in prose to convey a simple meaning, but it has become one among the foremost instruments of poetry in Western Europe, due to its former association with music.

Many centuries having passed, and cavemen being now mostly employed as football hooligans, even the art of conveying meanings by sheer sound has somewhat evolved; however, its original, imitative form often surfaces. The futurist movement, which thought mechanical noises were the sweetest melody, produced several pieces meant to whirr and rumble; here is the beginning of F. T. Marinetti's ode to a racing car:

> Veemente dio d'una razza d'acciaio,
> Automobile ebbrrra di spazio,
> che scalpiti e frrremi d'angoscia
> rodendo il morso con striduli denti

> *Vehement god of a steely race,*
> *car drunk on space,*
> *raring and writhing with anguish*
> *gnawing your bit with shrieking teeth*

Two things are remarkable in this piece: first, Marinetti multiplies the Rs in some words to create the effect of a revving of engines, and second, he associates them with unvoiced consonants, which sound 'inhuman'; a similar example in classic poetry is this line of Racine's, also quoted by Lausberg:

> pour qui **s**ont **c**es **s**erpents qui **s**ifflent **s**ur vos têtes?

in which the abundance of phonetic Ss, coupled with the Fs of the central 'sifflent' produces a distinct sensation of reptiles slithering around. As with most poetic techniques, English evidence is hard to find; however, still on the subject of snakes, here is something by D. H. Lawrence:

> And trailed his yellow-brown **slack**ness **soft**-bellied down, over
> the edge of the **stone** trough
> and rested his throat upon the **stone** bottom,
> and where the water had dripped from the tap, in a small
> clearness,
> He sipped with his **straight** mouth,
> **Soft**ly drank through his **straight** gums, into his **slack** long body

> .   .   .   .

Notice how Lawrence doesn't achieve the effect through simple homoeoprophoron, as most poets would do, but through geminatio: there are keywords, and these are repeated twice (or more), just as in Apollinaire's 'Les Colchiques' (see Chapter VII): in this part of the poem, where the animal is actually described in its most serpentine actions, *all* keywords begin with an S.

There are, of course, cases of *explicit* onomatopoea (things like 'and the dog went bark, bark'), even by such authors as Shakespeare and Eliot, not to mention Poe, but these are generally too trivial to be quoted.

More Subtle Effects

VOYELLES

A noir, E blanc, I rouge, U vert, O bleu: voyelles,
Je dirai quelque jour vos naissances latentes:
A, noir corset velu des mouches éclatantes
Qui bombinent autour des puanteurs cruelles,

Golfes d'ombre; E, candeurs des vapeurs et des tentes,
Lances des glaciers fiers, rois blancs, frissons d'ombelles;
I, pourpres, sang craché, rire des lèvres belles
Dans la colère ou les ivresses pénitentes;

U, cycles, vibrements divins des mers virides,
Paix des pâtis semés d'animaux, paix des rides
Que l'alchimie imprime aux grands fronts studieux;

O, suprême Clairon plein des strideurs étranges,
Silences traversés des Mondes et des Anges:
O l'Oméga, rayon violet de ses Yeux!
—Arthur Rimbaud

VOWELS

Black A, white E, red I, green U, blue O: vowels,
someday I shall talk about your latent births:
A, black velvety corset of resounding flies
that buzz around cruel stenches,

gulfs of shade; E, whiteness of vapours and tents
spears of haughty glaziers, white kings, shivers of umbels;
I, Tyrian purple, spat blood, laughter of fair lips
amidst wrath or penitential drunkenness;

U, cycles, divine vibrations of viridian seas,
peace of pastures strewn with animals, peace in the wrinkles
that alchemy prints on the ample, studious forehead;

O, supreme Clarion full of strange screeches
Silences crossed by Worlds and by Angels:
O, the Omega, violet ray of His Eyes!

As the sonnet above dramatically demonstrates, the choice of sounds in poetry is not limited in its scope to imitating natural noises. There are quasi-mystical theories that actually think of connecting groups of sounds to unrelated abstract concept on a purely psychological basis (e.g., the *f+l* group would be associated to moving lights, something that a medic acquainted with flukes and flatulence would strongly disagree upon), and it is with great pleasure that we dismiss these as preposterous. But it is a fact, and one proven by thousands of examples, that there is a correlation between phonetics and psychology of communication: anyone could quite see that the Italian word 'bacio' (in which the first consonant is pronounced with the lips, and the second forces the speaker to disclose them more) is more effective than the English word 'kiss' (in which the first consonant has the speaker open his mouth and bare his teeth, while the second makes him look as if he were growling) in conveying an amorous thought. Following this concept, based mostly on how the air touches one's vocal organs when sounds are pronounced, poets have built, since the earliest ages, a sort of palette from which vowels and, more often, consonants are chosen according to the mood of their work. The simplified version of this concept gives rise to the popular terms of euphony and cacophony; what is often labelled as the latter is an attempt at describing unpleasant realities; Arnaut Daniel, in a piece in which he defends a knight refusing a sexual practice he finds repulsive[g], starts:

Pus Raimons e Truc Malecx
chapten n'Enan e sos decx,
e ieu serai vielhs e senecx
ans que m'acort in aital precx
don puesca venir tan grans pecx:
al cornar l'agra mestiers becx
ab que traisses del corn lo grecx;
e pueis pogra leu venir secx
que'l fums es fortz qu'ieis d'inz des plecx.

Here the masculine 'ECX' rhyme creates the effect of someone sneering at the end of each line; the one-stanza-one-rime choice enforces this, and so does the fact that several line endings are spondaic, forcing the reader to stop as if disgusted before the last word (this is actually a rhythmic device as described below).

E. Pound, in his Canto XLV, already quoted several times, uses the archaic -TH endings and several other means in order to show how usury affects economy (all right, all right, I admit the subject is just as unpoetic as it might get) by making the verses flow in a hindered, irksome way:

> Usura rusteth the chisel
> It rusteth the craft and the craftsman
> It gnaweth the thread in the loom
> None learneth to weave gold in her pattern;

Baudelaire, and other symbolist poets achieve the same effect through nasal sounds; the reader can find examples of this in a multitude of works.

On the other hand, some schools of poetry, the first of which was perhaps that of the 'Dolce Stil Novo' (sweet new style) in thirteenth century Tuscany, believed that only love matters were worthy of being treated (which is a bit limited, but still a great deal more interesting than economy in the Middle Ages, if you ask me), and that this should be done by using sounds that rolled easily off the tongue and were pleasing to the ear. It was the first systematic application of what later came to be termed euphony, and which some poets, most notably Shelley, applied in a rather foolish way to just everything. Here is an example by the Dolce Stil Novo master Cino da Pistoia (the form, an Italian ballad, is, everywhere else, rare and obscure, and has not been described in this manual):

> Poi che saziar non posso gli occhi miei
> di guardare a madonna suo bel viso,
> mireròl tanto fiso,
> che diverrò beato lei guardando.
>
> A guisa d'angel che di sua natura,
> stando su in altura,
> diven beato sol vedendo Dio,
> così, essendo umana creatura,
> guardando la figura
> di quella donna che tene 'l cor mio,
> porria beato divenir qui io:
> tant'è la sua vertù che spande e porge,
> avegna non la scorge
> se non chi lei onora desïando.

Since I can't sate my eyes
with looking at my lady's beautiful face
I'll stare at it so intently
That I'll become blessed by looking at her.

In the guise of an angel who, by nature,
being in high [Heaven]
becomes blissful just by seeing God,
the same way I, being a human creature,
looking at the shape
of that woman that holds my heart
I could become blissful down here:
So great is the worth she irradiates and offers
That it happens that nobody can appreciate it
Unless he longingly honours her.

Cino tries to create a sensation of beatitude mostly by multiplying the diphthongs, and by avoiding the harsh sonority created by double consonants or by groups of them. Another typical rule of thumb used in this kind of writing is favouring certain sounds (typically, [b], [l], [m], [v]) and shunning others (typically,[k], [s] and those produced by the TH group); Cino doesn't really do that here, and uses words such as 'stando'.

As hinted above, some prudence should be used in moving from one language to the other; the R sound, for example, is only apparently the same in different languages: it actually is a very light, endearing sound in French (it's one of the *actual* reasons why most men find French girls sexy), a fairly neutral one in English and a forbiddingly harsh one in Italian. Furthermore, what we could term 'phonetic extremes', the sounds that are most difficult to pronounce, are generally limited to few languages: the TH of English does not exist in Italian, French or Provençal, and it is slightly different in Spanish; the -GL- sound of Italian is stronger than French or Spanish -ILL-, and has no equivalent whatsoever in English; twined consonants are actually pronounced as such in Italian only, and so forth.

Things are even more complicated when it comes to vowels: the A existing in most languages in the world, the 'velvety corset of resounding flies' of Rimbaud, does not exist in English (some say it corresponds to the U sound in, say, 'cut', betokening that they are either deaf of very stupid); the 'I' is different, double vowels are endemic of a few northern European languages, nasal ones exist in French but not in Provençal, in Portuguese but not in Spanish, in Icelandic but not in Danish, and so forth.

A good phonetics book (e.g., Lausberg's) can enlighten the Reader more about this quite confusing point, which would, again, exceed the scope of this work; on the other hand, anyone familiar enough with his own language certainly doesn't need to be told which sounds are harsh and which are not. As for people who are *not* familiar with the language they read, they should at least be aware that they are going to miss more than they think.

It is now interesting to consider a further example, and a British one at that, to see *how* the 'right' sounds are exploited. It is actually very difficult to entirely eliminate a series of words in favour of others, while it is more reasonable to highlight the phonemes through their involvement in homoeoprophoron or their position in the verse.

> Piping down the valleys wild
> piping songs of pleasant glee
> On a cloud I saw a child
> And he laughing said to me

This first stanza of Blake's introduction to *Songs of Innocence* is much based on Ls (and on the fairly neutral Ps) and contains a relatively huge number of diphthongs; the effect is that of a piece that could be read even by a child who isn't able to say all words properly. Note how this is achieved both by homoeoprophoron and lipograms (neither the short U nor the schwa appear in this stanza).

Rhythm and Effect

If one cares to reread the related chapter, he'll notice two things about classic verse:

- it grants the writer a good deal of freedom

- where it does not, it imposes obvious, mechanical conditions

This, of course, is not the beginning of one of those tales, told by an idiot, full of sound and fury, signifying that one should move on to free verse. It is just the due introduction to the fact that, in classic or in free verse, there is ample room for creating certain effects not only through the phonetic features of a given language, but also through the arrangement of stresses throughout the lines. Often, the two are combined, as in the Pound and

Arnaut Daniel fragments above. As it was for vowels and consonants, it'd be pointless to try to substitute the Reader's common sense and to describe all the possible patterns: only a few examples will be given to illustrate the point. This is fairly easy, as modern poetry actually has cases in which sequences of stressed and unstressed syllables are the only recognisable reoccurring feature of a poem (conventions are set as in Chapter II):

LOS ÁNGELES MOHOSOS

Hubo luz que trajo **UUSUSU**
por hueso_un almendra_amarga. US**UUSUSU**

Voz que por sonido, **SUUUSU**
el fleco de la lluvia, U**SUUUSU**
cortado por un hacha. U**SUUUSU**

Alma que por cuerpo, **SUUUSU**
la funda de aire USUUSU
de una doble_espada. UUUSUSU

Venas que por sangre, **SUUUSU**
yel de mirra_y de retama. UU**SUUUSU**

Cuerpo que por alma **SUUUSU**
el vacío, nada. **UUSUSU**
                                    —Rafael Alberti

THE MOULDY ANGELS

There was a light that had,
for a bone, a bitter almond.

A voice that, for a sound,
the fringe of the rain,
curtailed by an axe.

A soul that, for a body,
the airy sheath
of a double-edged sword.

Veins that, for blood,
gall of myrrh and of broom

Body that, for a soul,
the void, nothing.

The structure of this poem is rather complex, but what the ear immediately perceives is that eleven of the twelve lines end with either of the two patterns UUSUSU or SUUUSU (which, besides, resemble each other). The only exception cleaves the piece in two just after the first occurrence of the words 'cuerpo' and 'alma', that appear again just before the ending. The global result is oddly reminiscent of a rondeau, with its lines divided into two groups of rhymes (replaced here by the end-patterns) and its repeated hemistich (replaced by the double iteratio).

There is nothing new in the technique except for the fact it is actually applied to a good poem; for centuries, in fact, poetasters of all sorts have practised what is sometimes called barbaric meter, that is, the application of Grecian stanzas to modern languages. Since typical Grecian verses have fixed stress patterns, at least in some lines, the effect of this is similar to that of the piece above. Perhaps the most extensive attempt at this outside English, Latin and Greek, is the collection called *Odi barbare*, written in Italy by a pompous, patriotic fool called Carducci (who, as all pompous, patriotic fools, wallows in undeserved fame); here is the introduction (the rest is even sillier):

> Odio l'usata poesia: concede SUUSU UUSUUSU
> comoda al vulgo i flosci fianchi e senza SUUSU SUSUSU
> palpiti sotto i consueti amplessi SUUSU USUSU
> stendesi e dorme. SUUSU
>
> A me la strofa vigile e balzante USUSU SUUUSU
> co 'l plauso e 'l piede ritmico ne' cori: USUSU SUUUSU
> per l'ala a volo io còlgola, si volge USUSU SUUUSU
> ella e repugna SUUSU
>
> Tal fra le strette d'amator silvano SUUSUUUSUSU
> torcesi un'evia su 'l nevoso Edone SUUSUUUSUSU
> più belli i vezzi del fiorente petto SUUSUUUSUSU
> saltan compressi, SUUSU
>
> e baci e strilli su l'accesa bocca USU SUUUSUSU
> mesconsi: ride la marmorea fronte SUU SUUUSUSU
> al sole, effuse in lunga onda le chiome USUSUSUSUUSU
> fremono a' venti. SUUSU
>
> *I hate the usual poetry: it gives,*
> *comfortably, to the people her sagging hips and, without*
> *emotion, under the usual embraces,*
> *lies down and sleeps.*

Give me the watchful, springing strophe
with the applause and the rhythmic foot in the chorus:
I take her by the wing while she flies, she turns
and winces.

Such as, amidst the hugs of a sylvan lover
a maenad turns away on the snowy Thracian mount,
more beautiful the quirks on the flourishing breast,
when repressed, spring

and kisses and cries on the flushed mouth
are mixed: the marble forehead laughs
in the sun, loose in a long wave the hair
shakes in the wind.

English poetry has always been proud of being barbaric, so that this approach has been adopted from the beginning: an iambic pentameter, in its dullest, most literal form, is a sequence of equal USUSUSUSUS[U][U] patterns, as are the other examples of versification based on feet described in chapter I, the problem with it being that strictly single-pattern lines are just as trite, repetitive and, in the end, as tedious as their single-rhyme counterparts.

As with sounds, it is legitimate to wonder whether a particular rhythmic pattern can be associated to the imitation of natural phenomena or to a particular psychological state; this is a subtle question, and the answer is probably no. However, rhythms can be *combined* with accurate phonetic choices and used to strengthen their meaning. An easy parallel is the one with music: the length and volume of notes are fundamental, but it is very hard to write a minuet for drums.

We have seen before, especially with the homoeoprophoron, how this can be done; it is worth mentioning that the most common exercise of all, especially among overly pelagic authors, is trying to use language to imitate the ebb and tide of the sea. Among the many that did it are an apocryphal Raimbaut de Vaqueiras, Neruda, and Derek Walcott, whose 'A Sea-Chantey' is concluded by a threefold repetition of the verse:

The amen of calm waters

Here the short, stressed vowel of 'amen' suggests a wave breaking, the two long ones of 'calm' and 'waters' suggest one retreating. As in ancient poetry, more than the actual arrangement of stressed and unstressed syllables (which is still crucial to the effect), it is the length of the vowels that is of paramount importance; this is a feature of the English language that should have been considered more, especially by those who raved about Endymions, Adonaises and Chapman's Homers: but the dead cannot emend their stupidity.

Wonders can be done, however, even with Romance languages, in which all vowels are short: Antonio Machado manages to somewhat recreate the exasperating, intermittent buzzing of flies in his 'Las moscas':

> Vosostras, las familiares,
> inevitabiles golosas
> vosostras, moscas vulgares
> me evocáis todas las cosas.
>
> ¡Oh, viejas moscas voraces
> como abejas en abril,
> viejas moscas pertinaces
> sobre mi calva infantil!
>
> ¡Moscas del premier hastío
> en el salón familiar
> las claras tardes de estío
> en que yo empecé a soñar!
>
> [to be continued]

Pie Quebrado

A last thing worth mentioning before calling it a day is how, especially in a rhymed piece, the alternation of different verse lengths affects the general idea of a poem. Breaking the regularity of successions of long verses with shorter ones is one of the oldest habits of classical poetry. In Spain, already in the thirteenth century there were pieces in which octasyllabic lines were interrupted by tetrasyllabic ones; these are called 'pies quebrados' (literally, 'broken feet'). Their application is still alive today; a pie quebrado sounds sudden, if not snappish: here is the next stanza of 'Las moscas':

Y en la aborrecida escuela,
raudas moscas divertidas
perseguidas
por amor de lo que vuela

– que todo es volar – sonoras,
rebotando en los cristales
en los días otoñales...
Moscas de todas las horas

de infancia y adolescencia,
de mi juventud dorada;
de esta segunda inociencia,
que da en no creer en nada,

de siempre...Moscas vulgares,
de puro familiares
no tendréis digno cantor:
yo no sé que os habéis posado

sobre el juguete encantado
sobre el librote cerrado,
sobre la carta de amor,
sobre los párpados yertos
de los muertos.

Inevitables golosas,
que ni labráis como abejas,
ni brilláis como mariposas;
pequeñitas, revoltosas,
vosostras, amigas viejas,
me evocáis todas las cosas.

You, familiar,
inevitable gluttons
you, ordinary flies,
remind me of everything.

Oh, you old flies, voracious
as April bees,
old flies, persistent
over my infantile baldness!

Flies of the first tedium
in the family parlour,
[during] the clear Summer evenings
in which I began to dream!

And in the abhorred school,
swift, amused flies
pursued
out of love of that which flies

- since everything is flying- noisy,
resounding in the glasses
during the Autumn days...
Flies of every moment

of infancy and of adolescence,
of my golden youth;
of this second innocence
that comes close to not believing in anything,

of every time...Ordinary flies,
who, out of sheer familiarity,
won't have a worthy singer:
I don't know whether you have rested

on the enchanted toy
on the closed tome
on the love letter
on the open eyelids
of the dead.

Inevitable gluttons
that neither work like bees
nor glitter like butterflies;
rebellious little ones,
you, old friends,
remind me of everything.

Other languages have 'established' ways of doing the same thing. In Italian the endecasillabi are customarily mixed with lines of six metric syllables, French has the rondeau form and even in English Donne fittingly uses it, among others, in 'Womans Constancy':

Now thou hast lov'd me one whole day,
To morrow when thou leav'st, what wilt thou say?
Wilt thou then Antedate some new made vow?
Or say that now
We are not just those persons, which we were?
Or, that oathes made in reverential feare
Of Love, and his wrath, any may forsweare?
Or, as true deaths, true maryages untie,
So lovers contracts, images of those,
Binde but till sleep, deaths image, them unloose?
Or, your owne end to Justifie,
For having purpos'd change, and falsehoood; you
Can have no way but falsehood to be true?
Vaine lunatique, against these scapes I could
Dispute, and conquer, if I would,
Which I abstaine to doe,
For by to morrow, I may thinke so too.

This example is particularly ingenious because of the irregular pattern that matches the fickleness of the poet's mistress; in particular the four-syllables line, of Spanish origin, comes to highlight a sudden change of mind.

Note also how a long verse after a sequence of short ones has the effect of a comment, especially if it concludes a piece or stanza. As such it is used not only by Donne, but also in all of Spenser's *Faerie Queene*.

Now, Kind Reader, you who have followed me for so long through my toil, I release you: go and write or, if such is not your call, go and read, teach or sleep metrically sound dreams. Conclusions are not for the enlightened to read: they are but a paltry thing, meant for perfectionists and editors, and those that just can't get enough of our idiosyncratic writing. Are you one? Why, then Ile fit you (you merely have to turn the page).

Sources and further reading

Many of the books mentioned in the corresponding section of the preceding chapter are valid for this one as well, especially Jakobson's; one can integrate those with Ladefoged, P. *Vowels and Consonants*. (Oxford: Blackwell, 2001), which also has what all phonetics books should have: an attached CD (ROM). Many other treatises, especially in English, are concerned with poetic rhythm, at least in intention (many step way off the topic); among these Attridge, D. *Poetic Rhythm: An Introduction* (Cambridge: Cambridge University Press, 1995) stands like a beacon of sorts; Cetti, C. *Il ritmo in poesia: teorica razionale*. (Como: E. Cavalleri, 1938), although definitely outdated, is still somewhat interesting.

More information on the riches of modern Spanish poetry can be extracted from López Estrada, F. *Métrica española del siglo XX* (Madrid: Gredos, 1969) and from Areta Marigo, G.; Le Corre, H.; Suarez, M.; and Vives, D., ed. *Poesia hispanoamericana: ritmo(s)/metricas(s)/ruptura(s)* (Madrid: Verbum, 1999).

The Futurist movement, short lived, often funny and invariably silly is well outlined by Marinetti's many manifestos and declarations, collected in Marinetti, F. T. et al. *I manifesti del futurismo* (Firenze: Edizioni di Lacerba, 1914); he wasn't the only Italian poet who, not sated by his own works alone, felt compelled to theorise: this lamentable planet is also afflicted by Carducci, G. *La poesia barbara nei secoli XV e XVI* (Bologna: N. Zanichelli, 1881).

Torrents of ink have been poured, in Italy at least, on the subject of the Dolce Stil Novo; actually Dante, who adhered to the movement for a few years, was among the first to theorise about poetry in his *De vulgari eloquentia* (Forlì: the press hadn't been invented yet, sorry, 1305), while among the many modern authors that followed in his footsteps is Figurelli, F. *Il dolce stil novo* (Napoli : Ricciardi, 1933).

Conclusions

It is a widespread opinion that Fermi believed atomic power would improve the state of humanity rather than destroy part of it. Likewise, the Present Author, who has written this guide for his own amusement and his Readers', sincerely hopes it will never be employed as a means of oppressing students. There are, however, reasons to doubt this: permission to hand out copies of some chapters was asked for by staff members of the University of Arkansas, for instance.

If it were not so, this chapter would be useless: having a declaration of intents at the beginning is, in the Present Author's opinion, reason enough not to have a conclusion: either the writer has given what he has promised, and therefore you can complacently position the book on its shelf, or he hasn't, and you shouldn't pander to his fickleness by reading any further.

But students don't have this choice: they have to read on and they crave for a summary; so *Ile fit* them, too.

To summarise, a main point should emerge from this treatise: that very little in English poetry is indigenous. Its poetic forms are, with very few exceptions, first sifted through French and then imported; rhyme itself is a foreign device, and syllabic versification is clearly a Romance heritage.

This said, it is also rather evident that English poets have always had a hard time following whatever form they chose, and the most sophisticated means of expression employed in other languages, such as the rondeau and the so-called Petrarchan sonnet are only sporadic occurrences in this language. There is, in fact, somewhat of a friction between the nature of English and the Continental origin of its prosody, and this fact certainly abets the many that protest against its 'constrictions'. But what parts English from Romance languages, or from Old Norse, in phonetic terms? Only a linguist could, of course, answer a question like this in exact terms, but some features stand out even for the layman to see. The most evident feature is in the comparative abundance of phonemes: in English there are 22 vowel sounds (assuming the Reader speaks the modern version of the King's English, as the number varies according to the dialect considered), while in Provençal, the language in which the first rhymes were written, there are only eight and in Italian seven. French has seventeen, and it is interesting to notice that France is the homeland of the lipogram, a device (described in Chapter VII) which reduces them to a number closer to the southern Romance tongues.

On the other hand, most Western European languages seem to have similar sets of consonants; this would suggest that poetry based on assonance can be transferred only with great difficulty, while poetry relying on consonance or alliteration has a wider range of application: as a matter of fact, English has systematically rejected one of the most common Spanish writing styles, that based on assonance (see Chapter II), while it once adopted, and is now rediscovering, alliterative poetry (see Chapters V and VI).

Another characteristic of the English language is the fact that it is *stress-timed*, while most, if not all, romance languages are *syllable-timed*. This is quite a recent discovery, of which Chaucer, regretfully, couldn't have been properly aware. Simply put, it means that the time one takes to read an Italian verse depends roughly on the number of syllables therein contained, while for an English verse it depends on how many of them are stressed. This is no slight difference: poetry from the early Middle Ages was sung to music (usually readapted Gregorian chants), so that the underlying melody controlled its flow in time very strictly. In the transition towards 'spoken' poems in Southern France, writing verses with a set number of syllables also meant giving them an even duration. In order to obtain the same effect in English and, presumably, in Old Norse, one has to use a fixed number of stresses, which is exactly the case in the Nordic fornyrðislag adopted by many Old and Middle English writers. In this light, the key to alliterative poetry becomes the fixed number of stresses rather than the alliterations, and therefore one can see how its contemporary readers could accept the 'sloppy' style of the Exeter riddle in Chapter VI. Furthermore, one can also see why soon after the introduction of syllabic verses in England, came the invention and the immediate popularity of the iambic pentameter: it was an attempt at re-establishing the time-measure of the line, as were all uses of 'feet'.

It was only much later (in the eighteenth century) that English verse was re-interpreted in terms of Greek and Latin metres, with results that are some-times interesting, sometimes pathetic (iambic verses, for example, the basis of elegiac poetry in England are used almost only in farce in Latin).

Other similarities don't have the same rigorous factual base, but can be drawn from examples; one could wonder, for instance, what the English equivalent of a triolet is. We have seen in Chapter III that this form is mostly used in France for humorous poetry, but the few English examples known seem to safely deny this could be the case in English: whoever tries writing a triolet in this language is more than likely to be in the bleakest of moods. But let us take this quite typical triolet by Banville ('Opinion sur Henri de La Madelène', from *Odes funambulesques*):

> J'adore assez le grand Lama,
> Mais j'aime mieux La Madelène.
> Avec sa robe qu'on lama
> J'adore assez le grand Lama.
>
> Mais La Madelène en l'âme a
> Bien mieux que ce damas de laine.
> J'adore assez le grand Lama,
> Mais j'aime mieux La Madelène.

> *I love the Dalai Lama enough*
> *But I like La Madelène better*
> *With his lamé robe*
> *I love the Dalai Lama enough.*
>
> *But La Madelène has in his mind*
> *Things far better than that woolen damask.*
> *I love the Dalai Lama enoough*
> *But I like La Madelène better.*

Let us compare it, rather than with an English triolet, with this 1924 limerick by the anonymous 'Princeton Tiger':

> There once was a man from Nantucket,
> Who kept all of his cash in a bucket,
> But his daughter, named Nan,
> Ran away with a man,
> And as for the bucket, Nantucket.

In spite of Banville's greater skill in handling the task, there is a clear analogy between the techniques employed: where the triolet uses the paragram, 'damas de laine' to make 'La Madelène' stand out more, the limerick has the resonance 'Nan' to highlight 'Nantucket'; both use homophony, one implicitly in 'Nantucket'/'Nan took it' (faulty as it may be), the other in 'Lama'/'l'âme a'. Furthermore (and this is generally true), there are five *different* lines in a triolet, as in a limerick, and they are split in two rhyme groups, one of two and one of three elements, as in a limerick. The difference is in the fact that a triolet is 'stiffened' formally by the repeated lines, while a limerick is made 'rigid' by the forced stress pattern. Both forms are generally made of short, rapid lines. Confronted by all this evidence, one might well assume that the two forms are the cross-language equivalent of each other, and surmise that they would probably be put to the same use in their respective traditions. As with syllabic and alliterative verse, comparing how prosody is used in different languages enables us to draw comparisons between apparently unrelated devices.

It should be clear from the above, and from reading the various examples in the rest of this treatise, that prosody cannot be simply transferred from one language to another, and especially not from a Romance one to a Germanic one: in this light, Chaucer's attempt at borrowing all of French prosody at once, however supported by his own outstanding poetic skill, should be deemed imprudent, at best. Likewise, the many that believe the theory according to which English prosody descends directly from ancient Greek succeed in nothing but demonstrating that men descend from a tribe of peculiarly gullible baboons.

One very last example illustrates quite well the entire concept, and it is that of the sonnet: this canker of all poetry, according to some, evolved from a form called ghazal, which is still widely practised in Central Asia.

When the Arabs invaded Persia in 650 A.D., they introduced thereto a form called quasida, which the Persians customised into the ghazal (an adaptation to their tongue, according to the principles of this very book). When the Arabs invaded Sicily as well, in 827 A.D., their culture was permeated with Persian and they brought this new and improved version, the ghazal, there. When, eventually, a bored Norman emperor[h] in the 1230's made it so that one of the first poetic schools of Europe was started in the island, sonnets were one of the most commonly adopted forms there, and they were almost identical to those that would soon invade all Europe. This theory about the origin of the sonnet is not the only one (another one regards it as an atrophic involution of the Provençal song), but it is certainly the most suggestive: 'ghazal' means something like 'talking to women', which hints its purpose is the same as the first sonnets', whose aim was almost invariably getting into someone's pants. But this is basically the only thing the two metres have in common: the ghazal is an *open* form strongly segmented into couplets; the first two lines and each other one must end with the same word, while *internal* rhyme connects the first two lines with each other and with the second line of each couplet. The quasida, from which everything started, is even more different, being a type of extremely long poem in a single rhyme.

This shows again how successful adaptation to a new language can dramatically change the characteristics of a prosodic application in order to preserve its effect or its aim. We can even imagine some of the final stages of this transformation: the careful choice of the 14-line version of the ghazal, the removal of the end-word from each line, since the device is almost impossible to apply in Italian, and the subsequent creation of forms with a rhyme scheme AA BA CA DA EA FA GA (rare, but attested), their transformation into the typical Sicilian pattern AB AB AB AB CD CD CD and all the slow, patient filing of it into what we know today as sonnet.

Recent history shows instead how simple transplantation doesn't work at all: as a consequence of the Empire and of those ethnic affectations that characterise modern poetry, several British, and even Asian, poets have tried writing original ghazals in English. It has never worked.

This does not, of course, intend to be a eulogy of chauvinism: any literary tradition that finds itself isolated from the rest of the world falls into misery and withers in no time at all: the contempt of modern academies towards anything extra-national is one of the causes of the decadence of arts in the contemporary age. Even thinking that current prosody is 'already good enough' is preposterous: languages change continuously, and prosody should follow: as an example, the disappearance of feminine endings in French obviously carries with itself the loss of the rondeau redoublé and of a handful of other forms. On the other side, the sextain in Europe and the ghazal in Asia have been preserved unaltered for many centuries and are still valid forms of expression. The Reader should be aware that poetry, like every form of art, requires patience, experimentation and sensitivity in the development of its techniques; assuming otherwise means being an accomplice in the only crime no one care to seek justice for: its slow murder.

Sources and further reading

Readers wishing to learn more about the ghazal and other Asian forms should consult Thiesen, F. *Manual of Classical Persian Prosody with Chapters on Urdu, Karakhanidic and Ottoman Prosody* (Weisbaden: O. Harassowitz, 1982). Works in which the concepts of stress-timed and syllable-timed are explained are Abercrombie, D. *Elements of General Phonetics* (Edimburgh: Edimburgh University Press, 1967) and Roach, P. 'On the distinction between "stress-timed" and "syllable-timed" languages', in Crystal, D. ed. *Linguistic Controversies* (London: Edward Arnold, 1982). The influence of these concepts on verse has been sporadically considered; among the most interesting articles on the subject, see Hall, R. A., Jr. *Romance Philology* 19 (1965): 227 on old Spanish stress-timed verse. Information about the number of vowels and consonant sounds in a given language can be found in Crystal, D. *The Cambridge Encyclopedia of Language* (Cambridge: Cambridge University Press, 1987).

Endnotes

a   Cesar, calm Cesar, your foot on everything

b   Rainy, angry at the whole town

c   I have more memories than [I'd have] if I were a thousand years old

d   I am like the king of a rainy country

e   When the sky, low and heavy, weighs like a lid over the moaning spirit prey to interminable melancholia

f   My dirty old men! It's Salomé!

g   Anilingus

h   Frederick II (1194–1250)

Books Available from Gival Press

A Change of Heart by David Garrett Izzo
  1st edition, ISBN 1-928589-18-9, $20.00

  A historical novel about Aldous Huxley and his circle "astonishingly alive and accurate."
  — Roger Lathbury, George Mason University

An Interdisciplinary Introduction to Women's Studies Edited by Brianne Friel & Robert L. Giron
  1st edition, ISBN 1-928589-29-4, $25.00

  Winner of the 2005 DIY Book Award for Compilations/ Anthologies. A succinct collection of articles written for the college student of women's studies, covering a variety of disciplines from politics to philosophy.

Bones Washed With Wine: Flint Shards from Sussex and Bliss by Jeff Mann
  1st edition, ISBN 1-928589-14-6, $15.00

  A special collection of lyric intensity, including the 1999 Gival Press Poetry Award winning collection. Jeff Mann is "a poet to treasure both for the wealth of his language and the generosity of his spirit."
  — Edward Falco, author of *Acid*

Canciones para sola cuerda / Songs for a Single String by Jesús Gardea; English translation by Robert L. Giron
  1st edition, ISBN 1-928589-09-X, $15.00

  A moving collection of love poems, with echoes of *Neruda à la Mexicana* as Gardea writes about the primeval quest for the perfect woman. "The free verse...evokes the quality and forms of cante hondo, emphasizing the emotional interplay of human voice and guitar."
  — Elizabeth Huergo, Montgomery College

Dead Time / Tiempo muerto by Carlos Rubio
  1st edition, ISBN 1-928589-17-0, $21.00

  Winner of the Silver Award for Translation - 2003 *ForeWord Magazine*'s Book of the Year. This bilingual (English/Spanish) novel is "an unusual tale of love, hate, passion and revenge."
  — Karen Sealy, author of *The Eighth House*

Dervish by Gerard Wozek
1st edition, ISBN 1-928589-11-1, $15.00

Winner of the 2000 Gival Press Poetry Award. This rich whirl of the dervish traverses a grand expanse from bars to crazy dreams to fruition of desire. "By Jove, these poems shimmer."
— Gerry Gomez Pearlberg, author of *Mr. Bluebird*

Dreams and Other Ailments / Sueños y otros achaques by Teresa Bevin
1st edition, ISBN 1-928589-13-8, $21.00

Winner of the Bronze Award for Translation – 2001 *ForeWord Magazine*'s Book of the Year. A wonderful array of short stories about the fantasy of life and tragedy but filled with humor and hope. "*Dreams and Other Ailments* will lift your spirits."
— Lynne Greeley, The University of Vermont

The Gay Herman Melville Reader Edited by Ken Schellenberg
1st edition, ISBN 1-928589-19-7, $16.00

A superb selection of Melville's work. "Here in one anthology are the selections from which a serious argument can be made by both readers and scholars that a subtext exists that can be seen as homoerotic."
— David Garrett Izzo, author of *Christopher Isherwood: His Era, His Gang, and the Legacy of the Truly Strong Man*

The Great Canopy by Paula Goldman
1st edition, ISBN 1-928589-31-6, $15.00

Winner of the 2004 Gival Press Poetry Award. "Under this canopy we experience the physicality of the body through Goldman's wonderfully muscular verse as well the analytics of a mind that tackles the meaning of Orpheus or the notion of desire."
— Richard Jackson, author of *Half Lives, Heartwall,* and *Unauthorized Autobiography: New & Selected Poems*

Let Orpheus Take Your Hand by George Klawitter
1st edition, ISBN 1-928589-16-2, $15.00

Winner of the 2001 Gival Press Poetry Award. A thought provoking work that mixes the spiritual with stealthy desire, with Orpheus leading us out of the pit. "These poems present deliciously sly metaphors of the erotic life that keep one reading on, and chuckling with pleasure."
— Edward Field, author of *Stand Up, Friend, With Me*

Literatures of the African Diaspora by Yemi D. Ogunyemi
1st edition, ISBN 1-928589-22-7, $20.00

An important study of the influences in literatures of the world. "It, indeed, proves that African literatures are, without mincing words, a fountainhead of literary divergence."
—Joshua 'Kunle Awosan, University of Massachusetts Dartmouth.

Metamorphosis of the Serpent God by Robert L. Giron
1st edition, ISBN 1-928589-07-3, $12.00

"Robert Giron's biographical poetry embraces the past and the present, ethnic and sexual identity, themes both mythical and personal."
— *The Midwest Book Review*

Middlebrow Annoyances: American Drama in the 21st Century by Myles Weber
1st edition, ISBN 1-928589-20-0, $20.00

"Weber's intelligence and integrity are unsurpassed by anyone writing about the American theatre today..."
— John W. Crowley, The University of Alabama at Tuscaloosa

The Nature Sonnets by Jill Williams
1st edition, ISBN 1-928589-10-3, $8.95

An innovative collection of sonnets that speaks to the cycle of nature and life, crafted with wit and clarity. "Refreshing and pleasing."
— Miles David Moore, author of *The Bears of Paris*

Prosody in England and Elsewhere: A Comparative Approach by Leonardo Malcovati
1st edition, ISBN 1-928589-26-X, $20.00

"To write about the structure of poetry for a non-specialist audience takes a brave author. To do so in a way that is readable, in fact enjoyable, without sacrificing scholarly standards takes an accomplished author."
—Frank Anshen, State University of New York

Secret Memories / Recuerdos secretos by Carlos Rubio
1st edition, ISBN 1-928589-27-8, $21.00

"From the beginning, the reader feels pulled into the narrator's world and observes, along with him, a delicate, beautiful, and vulnerable universe as personal and intimate as a conversation between lovers."
— Hope Maxell Snyder, author of *Orange Wine*

The Smoke Week: Sept. 11-21, 2001 by Ellis Avery
  1st edition, ISBN 1-928589-24-3, $15.00

  Writer's Notes Magazine 2004 Book Award—Notable for Culture.
  Winner of the Ohioana Library Walter Rumsey Marvin Award
  "Here is Witness. Here is Testimony."
  — Maxine Hong Kingston, author of *The Fifth Book of Peace*

Songs for the Spirit by Robert L. Giron
  1st edition, ISBN 1-928589-08-1, $16.95

  This humanist psalter reflects a vision for the new millennium, one that speaks to readers regardless of their spiritual inclination. "This is an extraordinary book."
  — John Shelby Spong, author of *Why Christianity Must Change or Die: A Bishop Speaks to Believers in Exile*

Sweet to Burn by Beverly Burch
  1st edition, ISBN 1-928589-23-5, $15.00

  Winner of the 2004 Lambda Literary Foundation Award for Women's Poetry; Winner of the 2003 Gival Press Poetry Award
  "Novelistic in scope, but packing the emotional intensity of lyric poetry..."
  — Eloise Klein Healy, author of *Passing*

Tickets to a Closing Play by Janet I. Buck
  1st edition, ISBN 1-928589-25-1, $15.00

  Winner of the 2002 Gival Press Poetry Award
  "...this rich and vibrant collection of poetry [is] not only serious and insightful, but a sheer delight to read."
  — Jane Butkin Roth, editor, *We Used to Be Wives: Divorce Unveiled Through Poetry*

Wrestling with Wood by Robert L. Giron
  3rd edition, ISBN 1-928589-05-7, $5.95

  A chapbook of impressionist moods and feelings of a long-term relationship which ended in a tragic death. "Nuggets of truth and beauty sprout within our souls."
  — Teresa Bevin, author of *Havana Split*

Books for Children

Barnyard Buddies I by Pamela Brown; illustrations by Annie H. Hutchins
1st edition, ISBN 1-928589-15-4, $16.00

Thirteen stories filled with a cast of creative creatures both engaging and educational. "These stories in this series are delightful. They are wise little fables, and I found them fabulous."
— Robert Morgan, author of *This Rock* and *Gap Creek*

Barnyard Buddies II by Pamela Brown; illustrations by Annie H. Hutchins
1st edition, ISBN 1-928589-21-9, $16.00

"Children's literature which emphasizes good character development is a welcome addition to educators' as well as parents' resources."
— Susan McCravy, elementary school teacher

Tina Springs into Summer / Tina se lanza al verano by Teresa Bevin; illustrations by Perfecto Rodriguez
1st edition, ISBN 1-928589-28-6, $21.00

"This appealing book with its illustrations can serve as a wonderful learning tool for children in grades 3-6. Bevin clearly understands the thoughts, feelings, and typical behaviors of pre-teen youngsters from multi-cultural urban backgrounds...."
— Dr. Nancy Boyd Webb, Professor of Social Work, author and editor, *Play Therapy for Children in Crisis* and *Mass Trauma and Violence*

Inquiries: 703.351.0079
Books available via Ingram, the Internet, and other outlets.
Or Write :
Gival Press, LLC / PO Box 3812 / Arlington, VA 22203
Visit: *www.givalpress.com*

3283019

Made in the USA